CHRONICLES
of the
SALTER & DAVIES
FAMILY HISTORY

(13th to 20th century)

By

K.I.E. Salter-Davies

Chronicles of the Salter & Davies Family History 13th to 20th Century
First Edition
Published by DreamStar Books, May 2005
ISBN 1-904166-21-0

Lasyard House
Underhill Street
Bridgnorth
Shropshire
WV16 4BB
Tel: 0870 777 3339
e-mail: info@dreamstarbooks.com

Set in 'Garamond'

Printed and bound in Great Britain by Antony Rowe Ltd

Acknowledgements

John Christie-Miller of the Christie Hating Company
Shrewsbury Libraries – Helen Haynes
Mrs Page Life, Librarian of Davis Library, University of North Carolina, U.S.A;
Gloucester Record Office;
Gloucester Library;
Gloucester Family History Society;
Wotton-under-Edge Family History Society;
John Loosely of the Stroud Textile Society;
Hereford Record Office;
Hereford Library;
Cinderford Registrars Office;
Cinderford Library.
Coleford Library.
Miss Win Watkins (relative) of Coleford;
Molly Manifold (relative) of Coleford.
Brian Raymond of Coleford.
Ken Priske of Coleford.
The History Society of Frampton Cotterell
Maureen and Trevor Thompson of the Frampton Cotterell History Society.
Wiltshire Record Office;
Mrs Jenny; David and Dr. Barbara Carter of the Wiltshire Nimrod Indexes
Ken Rogers (Author) of Trowbridge, Wiltshire
Maureen Anderson of Stroud.
Eileen Bartlett of Buckinghamshire.
Cardiff Record Office, South Wales;
Newport Record Office, South Wales;
The Journal of the Webb One Name Register – "The Weaver";
Bristol Record Office;
Bristol Library;
Bristol Registrars Office;
Bristol and Avon Family History Society
Somerset and Dorset Family History Society;
Devon Family History Society;
Devon Record Office;
Devon Library at Exeter;
The Cathedral Archivist and Librarian, Devon.
Cornwall Family History Society
The Courtney Library & The Royal Cornwall Museum – Angela Broome

. John Salter (relative) of Epping, N.S.W. Australia.

. Steven Salter of Vancouver Canada

Jerry & Mary Adams, Latter Day Saints, USA

Rev. Phil Butcher of the Baptist Church in Wotton-under-Edge

Worcester and Droitwich Reference Library

Val Booler, Droitwich Library Manager

J.D. Hurst, author of 'Savouring the Past: the Droitwich Salt Industry'

David Hale of Gloucestershire

Contents

Introduction

Soon after my father's death and my early retirement (my mother having died some years earlier) I decided to sort out a box that contained my family archives. My mother, Rosalie Ellen, whose maiden name was Salter married my father, George Albert Davies, on the 24th November 1923. She gave to my care a number of photographs and other documents that relates to my family ancestry.

Since the beginning of my research I have endeavoured to bring together the occupational, religious, and social aspects of the family history and this includes the family names throughout the centuries from the present and as far back as the 11th century.

The family names, starting from the present 21st century are Francis, Gray, Buchanan, Evans, Williams, Robertson, Crowther, Farleigh, Saunders, Brown, Rossiter, Lea, Gillett, Davies, Hale, Salter, Leonard, Jancey (sometimes spelt Jauncey), Salisbury, Marsh, Whitaker, Manifold, Gwilliam, Watkins, Furney, Jones, Trotman, Webb, Peglar, Trull, Tipping, Cole, Bartlett, Fathers, Parker, Buller, Trethurffe, Courtenay, and Plantagenet.

It has been a tradition throughout the generations to include in the first names of some of the descendents the maiden name of the mothers parents as in William TRULL Salter whose grandmother was Mary (nee Trull) Salter. See pages 63-64. Another example was that of Richard TIPPING Salter. In this case the name Tipping was the maiden name of his grandmother Anne (nee Tipping) Trull. A second example is of John PETERSON Salter whose mothers maiden name was Peterson. My name, Keith Ivor Edmund Salter Davies is made up as follows. Keith is taken from "Dalkeith Place in Kettering" where my uncle Hubert Salter had his butcher's shops. Ivor was that of my father's family. Edmund was my great grandfather's name and Salter was the maiden name of my mother, Rosalie Ellen. The name Salter has recently been added to my first names in honour of my mother's family name.

The Salter surname originated from that of De Le Sel (De Selfac and sometimes spelt as Saltere). The 'e' in Saltere was eventually dropped and the surname is now generally spelt as Salter with some variations. I hope that my ancestors will forgive me for omitting some names but I know that the above names are belonging to my ancestral genealogical line.

I do not claim to be an expert in the various topics of this book and I therefore give some recommended readings for those who wish to study various aspects of the historical periods mentioned; i.e. the Salt Industry and the Wine Trade; The Woollen and Cloth Industries; the Weavers; Millers and Bakers; the beginning of Unionism; a change in Religious thought during the 17th and 18th centuries; the Chartists Riots; Hatters; and the dawn of the Industrial Revolution. It was a new era for the Salters, in that they changed their vocations and became tailors during the 19th century and beginning of the 20th century. However, they did retain their Religious Vocations. I must here give thanks to my cousin, Tyann (nee Salter) Leonard, who has helped me much in my research.

Pictures & Illustrations Index

Chapter One

A Brief History of the Salter's beginnings and their Forebears

1. The Salter's and the Early Years. 13th Century to the 15th Century.

The Salter family were first recorded in the reign of King John in the year 1211 as may be seen in the records of Shrewsbury Abbey. There is also mention in the Abbey records of 1272 where there is reference to John de Selfac, alias de Saltere, and his coat of arms is given in the Dunstable Roll of 1308. His Coat of Arms can be seen among others in the West Tower Window of Shrewsbury Abbey that is situated above the main entrance door of the Abbey.

The West Tower Entrance & Window of Shrewsbury Abbey

Humphrey Salter, the grandson of John de Selfac (de Saltere), was a Salt Manufacturer and he owned the salt brine spring country between Oswestry and Nantwich. He also owned property in Bader Street, Middle Street, Chirton Street, and Willow Street, Oswestry, Salop in 1393.

There is also a Thomas Salter who has mention in the Court Record of 1393 and 1399, Record 22 where Richard II witnessed deeds in 1429, 1430 and 1433.

From this period to the present day we find the family connected with Religion. Some found their vocations as Priests, Monks (who followed the rule of Saint Benedict) whilst others became Deacons and Lay preachers. Richard Salter, the grandson of Thomas, became Rector of Pontesbury, Salop in 1464; Rector of Stanlake, Oxon in 1473-1508; Rector of Whitfield, Northants, 1476-1482; Canon of Salisbury and Preb of Netherby in Terra, 1482-1508; Rector of Newington, Oxon, 1483; Canon of Lichfield and Preb. of Hansacre, 1489-1501; Chancellor of Lichfield and Preb of Alrewas, 1501-1505; Presenter of Lichfield and Preb of Bishop's Itchington, 1505-1519;Chaplain to Lionel Woodville, Bishop of Salisbury; Vicar General in Spirituals of the Bishop of Coventry and Lichfield, 1497. He built a house in the Close at Lichfield. He was educated at All Souls' College, Oxford and he became a Fellow in 1459; B.C.L. in 1452/3; D.C.L. in 1473. He died May 1519. Richard's brother, Robert Salter married Ankareta and he became the Bailiff of Oswestry. Their son, Robert, eventually settled in Dorset and his son William became Master in Chancery and he later bought 15 acres of land at Iver, Buckinghamshire in 1581. William was buried in the parish Church of Iver on the 13th November 1606.

2. Salter derived from the word Salt & the Flemish/Flanders connection

a) The name Salter is derived from the word 'Salt'. When Latin was the universal language it was sometimes spelt as Saltere, Saltern or Salte that translated into our present English language means Salt.

b) It has been suggested that the name de Selfac (de Saltere) originated from Northern France. Salter or Saltere has been noted as one of the names associated with immigrants to Essex from Flanders. However, the prefix 'de' before a name is of Latin/French origins and it would suggest therefore that this theory is correct especially when we take into consideration that William the Conqueror gave his faithful followers English lands in exchange for their loyal services.

3. William the Conquer

William the Conquerors fellow countrymen were given land-ownership in 1075. After defeating the English barons in 1066 he was invited to become King of England and therefore in order to secure his victory he encouraged his fellow Normans to remain loyal by granting land ownership within the realms of England. Land was split up into estates called 'Manors'. The Lords or Barons, in theory at least, were to show loyalty and obedience to the King and when the King required assistance to protect his realm, he would call on his Barons and he would expect military allegiance.

The Barons of the Manor would like wise parcel out parts of his land to his subordinates, his Vassals who were called 'Ceorls'.

The Court affairs were written in Latin and the spoken word in French; thus the words like county, village, justice, prison, money and rents are of French origin. The

Salters territorial possessions extended across from Oswestry to that of Nantwich and even as far north as Lancashire. We know with certainty that the Salter family, in the reign of King James was given land in 20 different counties throughout England in return for loans and favours offered to the King.

In 1140 more Jews were to enter England. In return for special favours they received protection from the King. The Jews, except for the Salters, were the only people to be permitted to trade as moneylenders or Pawnbrokers. In addition to their special treatment the Jews were allowed as Vassals to the Barons, to build stone houses within the realm. The Salters had become prosperous through the manufacture of Salt and Wine (the wine having been produced in Flanders) and as a result they were also permitted to become moneylenders. It has been recorded that the Salters were lending large sums of money to the Kings of England. King William had promised protection to the Jews and to some extent to the Salter families. King William's son Henry retained the philosophy by encouraging the colonization in England by his native Flemish Knights and Vassals. Henry was to grant lands in the hope that his followers would be beneficial to the trade in Agriculture, the Woollen Manufacture and the general trading links with the Continent.

4. Salt Production

In recent years there has been major archaeological discoveries in and around Droitwich in Worcestershire. These findings have given us an insight into the production of salt prior to the Middle Ages. Salt was a major commodity in the U.K. and it could be put as equal to the production of wool in the same periods. We know from archaeological finds that Salt was being produced as early as the Stone Age period. We also know that the Romans were producing Salt during the occupation (AD43 to 410) and Salt was produced in large quantities during the Anglo-Saxon period. Nevertheless, we can gleam from these discoveries in and around Droitwich and the river Salwarpe that the production of salt was procured by way of the 'Open Pan' method.

Salt was to form over millions of years, and when the rivers such as the Severn, the Teme, the Avon and the Salwarpe were to brake their banks the Salt from the sea waters (these rivers being tidal) was spread over the land. Over the years when the sea-water had evaporated it left deposits of Salt within the depths of the clay soil. Eventually streams were formed under ground and in later years Brine-Springs were to appear on the surface - Brine Springs being concentrated seawater salt

Due to the fact that Salt appeared initially close to the surface it was easily obtained. However, in later years the Salt had to be extracted from a deeper level under ground. In order to extract the Salt it became necessary to build a Well. These Wells were built of timber in a barrel shape, similar design to the spring water wells that may be seen all over the country to this day. Pumps were later used to extract the Brine from these Wells. When the Brine was extracted from the Wells it had to be allowed to evaporate in order to produce pure Salt residue. Natural evaporation in the U.K. was a slow process due to the mild climate and therefore it was necessary to quicken the process.

This was achieved by placing the Brine into containers made of durable wood and thus to heat it to form Salt Crystals. This would be transferred to another container in order for it to drain and as a result a solid block of Salt would form. About six containers would be placed on donkeys for the transportation of these blocks of Salt to various parts of the Country. This proved to be a profitable business in those days and as a result landowners became wealthy merchants who would travel to London, the Capital City, for the trading markets and possible for the export trade.

The following sketch is an example at to how Salt was produced in the 16th century and the tools used

Salt worker with implements from a 16th century German industrial treatise. The Droitwich salt worker used a very similar set of tools.

Medieval wooden implements from Upwich. Left: salt paddle used for stirring brine during boiling. Centre: mullet. Right: head of a salt rake used to bring salt to edge of pan during brine boiling.

Reproduced by kind permission of J.D. Hurst, author of 'Savouring the Past: the Droitwich Salt Industry'
Worcester County Council

5. Servants of the Crown

Some of the Salters became servants of the Crown. Sir Edward Salter became Page to Elizabeth I and later Carver to James I. A Carver was a person who would slice and cut meat with a large knife at a banquet. However, a Carver was also a Sculptor who was skilled in the art of engraving figures or figurines out of wood or ivory. Some of the family showed artistic flair in later generations. One such member of the family and a direct descendant of the Salters is that of John Davies whom had his Art exhibited in Manchester, 1940-1950.

George Salter of Dorset was granted in 1550 a coat of arms for services to the Crown. And George, a cousin of the said George of Dorset, occupied the seat at Denham Court and Manor, Buckinghamshire and he was the owner of several farms in Somerset and Dorset. This George was a London merchant and financier who lent £19,000 (a substantial sum of money in those days) to James I, and who in return received confiscated lands in 20 different Counties and in London, from the King. He was buried at Saint Dunstan-in-the-East on the 18th January 1607.

Another connection with Royalty was that of Mary Salter who married John Peeters of Horton on the 18th May 1623. John Peeters was the escort to Charles II, of whom he helped to escape at the Battle of Worcester.

Senior Members of the Salter Family remain in Northern Counties

During the later part of the 15th century, John Salter became Clerk of the Peace for the County of Salop. He died in 1492 and he is buried with his wife Isabella in the parish Church of Saint Nicholas, Newport in Salop. A brass plate is affixed to the wall in the Chancel and bears the inscription; 'Lo here lies entombed among ancient ashes John Salter, clerk of the peace; he gave his soul to Christ on the feast of Saint Mark in the year one thousand five hundred less eight. Near him in close company lies his wife Isabella herself, may the Creator of all things give them peace, Amen'. This brass plate was originally fixed to the floor of the Chancel. Their son John, who had studied law, became Sheriff of Shropshire in 1521 and he was a member of the Council in the Marches of Wales. He was also a Judge. He is also buried in this Church together with his wife. Their Tomb was originally placed in the Western end of the Nave. However, it was later moved and placed in the Chancel of the Church where it may be seen today. The tomb had been erected to his memory and consisted of a beautiful alabaster altar tomb with sculptured figures. These figures are, regrettably, now defaced. The figures of John and his wife are laid full length upon the top of this altar tomb. When the tomb was moved in 1828 they found underneath another remains of a woman. These remains could have been their daughter or a relative. She had a crucifix and Rosary beads around her neck. They had one child, Jane and this could have been her remains.

She firstly married Thomas Chetwynd of Newport Salop. After the death of Thomas she married Sir William Sneyd of Bradwell, Kent.

The Salter's Tomb in Saint Nicholas Church in Newport Salop

The family home is situated down the main road from the Church to the left by a garage. The name of the property was 'Salters Hall' in Salter Lane. As a result of Jane's marriage to Chetwynd the property passed to the Earls of Shrewsbury and it remained with them until 1830. John, the Earl of Shrewsbury eventually conveyed it to Dr. Milner who was a Roman Catholic. During this period, Mass and prayers were said in one of the rooms of Salter Hall. Salter Hall was later transferred to the use of the Catholic Church. Little of the old house remains, but the new building is now the Catholic Church of St. Peter and Paul, which also includes the Presbytery and the Old Salter Hall. In 1832, A.W. Pugin designed the new building. Pugin was also the Architect of Ratcliffe College in Leicester and Wadhurst in Surrey for the Rosminians.

Pugin designed the new building of Salter Hall in the Gothic style for Lord Shrewsbury. It is of red brick with stone dressings. In the west wall of the aisleless nave is a circular window and it is decorated with tracery. The porch to the Church was added in 1920. The Presbytery consists of four stone mullioned windows with square headed drip moulds. It is constructed of 2 storeys and the windows have parapet gables above. At the south end of the Presbytery one can identify the remains of the Old Salter Hall. However, the interior is much changed from that of the original design, and the old beams are the only means of identifying its age and past glory.

Saint Nicholas Church and Salter's Lane

Salter's Hall – now the Catholic Church of Saint Peter & Paul

A Plaque on the wall of St. Peter & Paul Catholic Church in Newport, Shropshire, reads:

"Salter's Hall

Sir John Salter, Lord Chief Justice for North Wales and Sheriff of Shropshire built the first recorded house in 1452. Little of this house remains, but an inglenook, a bolthole and, beneath the present roof; the roof timbers survive from a 17th century house, which was owned by the Chetwynd Family.

The first Catholic Licensed Chaplaincy in Shropshire was moved here from Longford Hall in 1789, and in 1832 the Church of Saints Peter and Paul was added. Salter's Hall was the seat of the first Catholic Bishop of Shrewsbury from 1851 to 1868"

Chapter Two

The Salter's Migrate to Various Parts of the UK. (1475)

By the end of the 15th Century the Salter's had become extensive landowners and prosperous from the manufacture of Salt in and around Shropshire; Cheshire; Staffordshire and Worcestershire. Some of the Salter's were also Wine Importers from the Continent. They were a large family about this time and they were ever increasing in numbers. The average number of children was eight. Multiply this by each generation and one can have some idea as to the growth of the family. It is feasible therefore that the reason, but not necessarily the main reasons, for the dispersal from Shropshire by some of the junior members of the family to various parts of the Country was to survive. They needed to find work and wealth elsewhere if they wanted to care for their family needs and to continue in prosperity. Nevertheless, some failed in later years to maintain their inherited wealth and prosperity especially where trade in the cloth industry declined. This was seen in the later part of the 18th and the early part of the 19th centuries, as was seen in the West Counties during the Textile crises.

The senior members of the family arranged a meeting in about 1475 to discuss what action should be taken to survive the conflicts of the Baronial small armies and the conflicts of the Royal Household for the Crown of England. Whose side should they be on – should it be the Lancastrian cause (the Red Rose) or should they be on the side of the Yorkists (the White Rose)? As is seen in many families there were differences of opinion. It was eventually decided to divide their wealth and go and seek their fortunes in other parts of the Country and to sow their seed. Another reason for dispersal would be to oversee the land that was given to the family by the King.

The Coat of Arms of the Salter family can be traced back to the reign of Edward I in 1300. The Arms of the senior branch are extremely rare, possibly unique. They consist of the Arms of one of the Salter's, Sir John Salter, who quartered his Sheriffs Arms with his family Arms. Subsequently these arms were borne by his brothers and nephews as well as by his son-in-law, who was of the family of Chetwynd of Ingestre Hall. The armorial bearings of the Salter family of Dorset and Somerset are exceptionally good example of differentiating.

The Following Sketches are some examples of Family Crests

Courtenay Coat of Arms of Devon

Salter Coat of Arms of Shrewsbury

Coat of Arms of George,
Second son of Robert Salter of Dorset

Coat of Arms of Sir Nicholas Salter,
Third son of Robert Salter

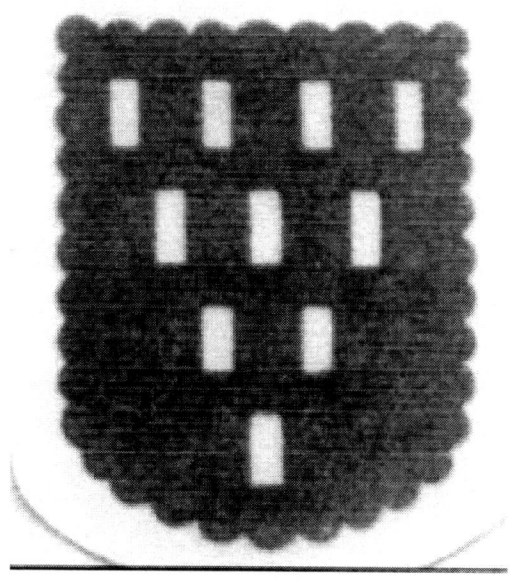

The Salter Coat of Arms of Devon

Coat of Arms of the Buller Family of Cornwall

Coats Of Arms Of The Bartlett Families Of Devon

John Adams Bartlett of Liverpool/Devon

William Bartlett of Teignmouth in Devon

The Wool Trade in the West Counties

Besides Salt manufacture there was the Wool trade. For over 300 years from King John in the 12th century to that of Henry VII in the 16th century we see Wool as being of equal prominence to that of Salt. Wool was a commodity that brought wealth to the nation.

Edward I was worried that his finances were at low ebb. He decided to have wool seized from merchants at the ports, including that of Bristol. He ordered his courtiers to find him provisions for a ship that was to carry him to Flanders. The wool trade with Flanders was good. He had also introduced a levy on wool in order to fill his purse. However, the Webb and Salter families were supported by the King and they did not have their merchandise seized. Perhaps this was due to the fact that Edward I had strong ties with the families of Trethurffe; Courtenay; Buller and Parker families.

While Edward 1 was out of the Country the Barons objected to the war with France. The Constable Bigod, the Earl of Norfolk, and Marshall Bohun, the Earl of Hereford, went to London to forbade the Kings Council to collect any of the moneys levied on wool. This levy was introduced in order to support the war machine. The Barons believed that the tax was unjust. Parliament was hastily summoned and it was agreed that the Great Charter of King John should be re-affirmed. A clause was added to the effect that the King was not to take "such manner of aids or prices save by the common assent of the realm; and that the 'Maltote' (the tax on wool) was to be forfeited. The King on his return agreed to this. The Barons had won their day and as a result Parliament was seen to be a power to be reckoned with. The Earl of Hereford, Bohun, was related to Elizabeth Courtenay of Devon by her first marriage.

Church & Politics

Church and Politics was not a thing to be admired by pious and holy men. However, the feudal system in England at this time, when William, a Flemish King, was eventually elected King of England and to be known as William I was enhanced throughout his rule. The Saxons had a similar system and therefore it was not altogether new to England.

There were land-less men, 'Villeins' who owed their allegiance to their tenants, known as 'Mesne-Tenants'. These in turn held their allegiance to the Greater-tenants-in-Chief, who was on the one side of the chain – Earls and Barons whilst on the other side were Abbots and Bishops. These two groups formed the Great Council of Landowners. They likewise were to show their allegiance to the King. The King was in possession and Sovereign of the whole lands of England.

Some of the Manors were leased to the Lesser-tenants-in-Chiefs and these consisted on the one hand the fighting men of England, the Kings Knights; whilst on the other side we see the Bailiffs farming the land on behalf of the King.

Because of this land ownership under the King we can see how rivalry between State and Religious houses could be a problem in later years.

Sketch of the Feudal System

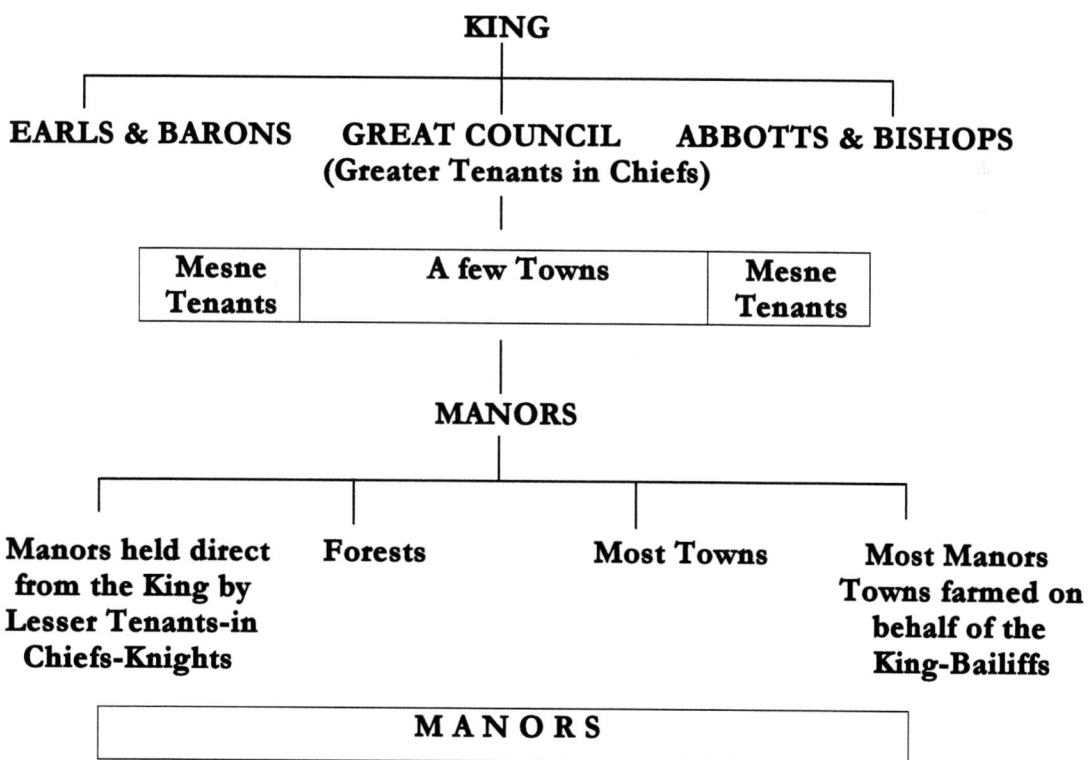

We see that it was not uncommon under this pyramid feudal system that even Bishops were to raise armies as in the case of King Williams' half-brother, Odo.

The Bishop wanted to wage war against Italy. This angered William, who put Odo in prison for the rest of his life.

Chapter Three

Salter's & Religion

We first hear of the Stewardship of the Salters in the archives of Shrewsbury Abbey. The first Church to be built on the site of the Abbey was a Wooden Chapel. It was built prior to the Norman Conquest of 1066. We have mention in Chapter one that the Salters were from the Continent and we can assume that the Salters were offered Manorial territory and that they were to become protectorates of the Crown as we see them to be in later generations under James I. In times of conflict the Barons would be called to arms to support the Crown. Although during this period the Barons were feuding amongst themselves and therefore not all remained loyal to the King.

Earl Roger of Montgomery who received the County of Shropshire in 1071 gave the Church to his clerk, Odelerius of Orleans who was the father of the historian Orderic Vitalis. His writings are recorded in the Doomesday Book. In February 1083, Earl Roger pledged that he would build a stone Abbey on the site by laying his gloves on the Altar of St. Peter.

The Salters once again have mention with regard to Shrewsbury Abbey. The Charltons of Apley became prominent as the protectors and managers of the Abbey Estates. John Charlton, Lord of Powys, had intervened to secure the appropriation of Condover Church in 1312, and in the early 16th century four of the family were active as stewards, and bailiffs. Some were to become Rent-collectors who drew pensions and liveries on the Abbey's Estates; namely, Sir William Charlton of Apley, his son Thomas, Richard and Francis Charlton. Sir William's cousin was John Salter who acted in the Council of the Marches and Richard Salter was to become Stewart of the Abbey under the Chief Steward, George, Earl of Shrewsbury. The Earl was most probably another cousin of the Charltons and therefore of the Salters. The Salter's residence was known as Salters Hall, Newport, Salop. This residence became the inheritance of the Earls of Shrewsbury in later years.

In the later part of the middle ages the community consisted of eighteen monks, one of whom was the Prior of Morville, and each of the senior monks held several offices. The Abbot in 1251 was to receive a Papal licence to wear the ring and in 1397 he was granted permission to use the mitre, ring and other pontifical insignia as is the custom to this present day. He may stand in for a Bishop in some instances. However, much of the records during this period have sadly been lost together with much of the Abbey's library. Some records may have fallen into private hands.

During the 14th century the Abbey was to see considerable change in structure under Abbot Nicholas Stevens. Unfortunately the Abbey was to be badly neglected after the Reformation. The Reformation caused many other Religious houses to suffer sacrilege and ruin, and never to be used again as a place of worship to God. It is true that there were many wrongs done under the roof of the house of God, but that did not warrant profanity where the wrongs of man were concerned. Any house of prayer is a sacred place when one is giving glory to our Father in heaven.

It may have been the results of the extensive alterations by Abbot Nicholas Stevens, that the Chapel of Saint Winifred was altered and a number of Sculptures were lost. However, in later years, fragments of a stone screen of about the same date suggest that the Chapel of St. Winifred stood on the north side of the nave, below the pointed arch of the arcade that faces the north porch. Stones with three sculptured figures, representing Saint John the Baptist; Saint Winifred; and Saint Bruno were found in a garden and they have been restored to their original position in the screen. There were two further restoration works carried out in the 19th century.

In 1540 the Abbey had two chimes, each of five bells, one in the western and one in the central tower. The largest bell, weighing 34 cwt., and known as Saint Winifred's Bell was in use until it cracked in 1730 and it was then melted down.

The Salters also have mention in the history of the Priory of Wombridge. The founders of the Augustinian Priory of Saint Leonard at Wombridge were Shropshire barons of middling rank and the modest scale of their possessions determined the size and endowment of their family monastery Chapels.

The Courtenay family of Devon, who would in later generations become related to the Salters by marriage, were to produce men of the cloth. William Courtenay became Archbishop of Canterbury from 1381 to 1396. He was Bishop of Hereford in 1370; Bishop of London in 1375; appointed Lord High Chancellor of England in 1381; and he officiated at the marriage of Richard II to Anne of Bohemia in 1382. It is feasible that Thomas Salter of whom has mention in Chapter One, had also been present at Richard II wedding. His Grace, William Courtenay, Archbishop of Canterbury, was later to crown the Queen. He was not afraid to speak out and in 1385 he publicly rebuked the King for his extravagance. As a result he was forced to return to Devon and to take refuge among his family Vassals and Retainers. However, in 1386 he was appointed by Parliament as one of the Commissioners to reform the Royal household. He later acted as mediator between the King and his enemies. He died on the 31st July 1396.

Richard Courtenay, a close and personal friend of King Henry V became Bishop of Norwich, 1413 – 1415. He was taken under the wing of his uncle, William, Archbishop of Canterbury of whom he received his education. His Uncle, William, left Richard his best Mitre in the event that he should become a Bishop – which he did. He became Chancellor of Oxford University in 1407.

Peter (known as Piers), the third son of Sir Phillip Courtenay of Powderham became Bishop of Exeter in 1478. His mother, Elizabeth, was the daughter of Walter, the 1st Lord Hungerford. Peter had plotted with the Duke of Buckingham against Richard 111 in 1484. In the same year he presented Exeter Cathedral with the great bell that was to be called 'Great Peter'. This bell was to be recast by Thomas Purdue in the late 17th century. The plot to overthrow the King failed and he fled into exile with his cousins Walter and Edward Courtenay (the husband of his niece, who was later to become the Earl of Devon.) He died in 1492. His ancestor, Hugh Courtenay, the 2nd Earl of Devon, died in 1377 and is buried in Exeter Cathedral alongside his wife, Margaret of Powderham Castle. Their alter tomb with their effigies may be seen in the Cathedral.

Exeter Cathedral

William Buller, D.D., a descendent of the Courtenay family through Margaret Trethurffe, who was the cousin and co-heir of the Earl of Devon, and who was to marry Richard Buller, became bishop of Exeter. William was born at Morval, Cornwall on the 20th August 1735. His wife Ann was the daughter of John Thomas, D.D., who was the Bishop of Winchester. William died 12th December 1796 and Ann died 28th August 1800, aged 63.

Catherine Buller, the daughter of Sir Richard Buller, the son of Francis Buller and the husband Alice Hayward, the daughter of Sir Rowland Hayward, was born in 1600 at Saint Stephens Church, near Saltash in Cornwall. She married James Parker of Warleggon on the 18th December 1617. Their daughter, Cordelia, was born about 1627, and she married Rev. John Fathers on the 19th May 1651. We will now be able to see the link between the Salter family and the above ancestors in the marriage of Katherine, the daughter of Rev. John and Cordelia Fathers, to Rev. James Salter of Devon. The marriage took place sometime between 1673/6.

Parish Church of Saint Stephen, near Saltash, in Cornwall

Pictures taken on 29th September 2002 of St. Stephen Church, near Saltash, in Cornwall

During this period of history, the incumbents of a particular parish were often appointed to other parishes that were a long distance apart. For example, Edward Salter who became curate of Shenfield, Essex in 1591 also became Rector of Monks Ellighe, Suffolk in 1595. He was granted arms on the 22nd May 1623. He was baptized on the 14th August 1564. He married Mary the daughter of George Nun of Felsham, Suffolk. He was educated at Pembroke College, Cambridge where he obtained a B.D.

Richard Salter who became Rector of Pontesbury, Salop in 1464 had also other parishes under his care. His father was William Salter who has mention in a deed relating to a shop in Le Ratinnowe, Oswestry. He later became Rector of Stanlake, Oxon between 1473 – 1508 and he was later to become Chaplain to Lionel Woodville, Bishop of Salisbury and Vicar General in Spirituals of the Bishop of Coventry and Lichfield in 1497. He also has mention in Chapter One. He died May 1519.

A Diocesan Visition by a Bishop

Throughout the generations the Bishops were and they are still responsible for the care of their flock within their jurisdiction, their Diocese. They would not only visit the various Parishes within the Diocese, but they would also visit the Religious houses.

In one such visitation by the Bishop to Shrewsbury Abbey he was to complain of a preoccupation with secular business. Brother Thomas of Broughton was forbidden to undertake secular business. This was between 1315 and 1316. However, by the year 1324 this brother was still holding the Courts of Roger Corbet. During this visitation the cellarer was found to be eating apart with guests in the Cellarium of the house. These occupations were to help keep the Abbey out of debt. Thomas Forster, in 1519 was able to lend money to the Abbot of Lilleshall in the sum of £40 over the period of four years. The resources were seen to be well organized and carefully used. In 1535, and after many of the Salter families had dispersed to various Counties within the U.K., the total gross revenue was said to be £72.15s.8d, of which temporalities accounted for £62.9s. The only fees then recorded were £1 to William Charlton, the Chief Steward. Richard Salter, the steward of the Courts, received 10s. However, the fees actually paid were in fact much higher. In 1536 William Charlton actually received £2 a year and the Salter's successor as auditor and clerk of the Courts were to receive £1. In addition three local bailiffs were paid 6s.8d. This sum was paid to the bailiff and rent collector in Oakengates.

The first Ministers' account for 1535 to 1536 brought the gross income of the priory at £89.3s.8d. This account also included receipts of £10.11s.4.received from the Wombridge demesnes that was omitted in the earlier assessment of accounts. By this date all the demesnes were let, except those at Wombridge, where an interesting feature of the economy was the use made of mineral resources. Coal was dug in two pits at Wombridge and this brought in another £5 per year income. There was also a small iron- work at Oakengates, which was described in 1535 as the 'Molendinum Ferrarium' that was worth 13s.4d. In 1536 a 'smithy' was let for £1.6s.8d. The total profits of coal and iron put together may seem a small amount but when we calculate the total percentage it amounted to some 7% of the income. The visitations between the years 1451 – 1524 were to show good returns and there was seen to be good discipline and the house in general appeared to be run in an orderly fashion.

Another such visitation was that of Bishop Stapledon of Exeter. This visitation took place in the reign of Edward II. Although the Bishop did not carry out the visitation himself, he arranged for the Chapter of Exeter Cathedral to send representatives on his behalf. They eventually sent Robert de Veteri Terra (He would be known today as Oldfield) and John of Uphaven. They were called Seneschals of the Chapter. During their visit they found some items missing. The report of this visit is as follows:

A Report on a visitation by the Seneschals of the Chapter

"A Chalice, gilt inside, sufficiently good; no PYX for the Eucharist, but a PYX for Altar-breads; a decent little PAX-board (the board of peace – this was passed to each other before communion). There was no vessel (PYX) for the visitation of the sick|; four cruets sufficiently good; a frontal at the high Altar, sufficiently good; a paschal candle; two processional candles; a processional cross in sufficient good order; two processional crosses of pewter; a chrismatory of wood with a lock."

They also found two sets of vestments, one for festal, and a second for ordinary days; there was four cloths for the Altar – however, it was said that two of these needed to be blessed. They found that one chasuble was sufficiently good whilst the other two were not in good condition. There was a Psalter that was badly worn and therefore unfit to use. Not only were these visitations to concern the Priest, but also to scrutinize the parishioners themselves. The reports that have been recorded would make good and interesting reading for those with an inquisitive mind and to those who desired to know how people spent their occupational, and leisure periods of the day, and to what extent did the environment shape their lives. This indeed would need another book if time would permit. It may also be worthy of note that since Vatican 11 the practice is to shake hands prior to communion as a sign of peace. The Monks themselves have always embraced each other before Communion as a sign of peace and goodwill.

A change in Religious Thought (late 17ᵗʰ to 18ᵗʰ century)

Before Henry VIII and his quarrel with Pope Leo X there were times when the Kings of England would repudiate the authority of the Papacy. William I, William Rufus II, and Henry I all had their differences with the Church and Pope.

Pope Gregory VII (Hilderbrand) was a reformer. He believed that the Church should be independent from Kings and Princes and free from State control. The big question was who should appoint a Bishop-should the King or the Church?

William I believed in the supremacy of the King in all affairs of State and Church. The King alone should be the ultimate decision maker within his realm. Pope Gregory VII was firm with other Princes but he showed tolerance with that of William I. He saw in him a stubborn man but a King who wanted only the good of the Church.

In contrast, William Rufus, the successor and heir, was keen on acquiring much wealth for himself, and with the help of Ramulf Flambard, his Justiciar, they saw in the Church a means of acquiring this wealth through the property of the Church. The Church, the Abbeys were wealthy Landowners and the Abbots and Bishops were very often from the nobility, the Landed Gentry. There arose a policy of keeping vacant a Church Office in order to obtain funds whilst the vacancy existed. Thus appointments of Abbots and Bishops by the King were not acceptable to the Pope who believed that the Church should hold this authority of appointments alone and free from state interference.

The Seeds of the Reformation

During King Stephens reign there arose the question of who should appoint a new Archbishop of Canterbury. This question was not new. It had previously involved William I and William Rufus. This would also cause problems between Church and State in future generations.

Whilst the barons were arguing amongst each other, the Church was steadily working towards independence from State and lay control. However, a compromise was to be reached in this instance. The elected Bishop would receive the ring of Office, the symbol of the union of Bishop and his flock, and the pastoral staff that represented the Bishops authority and care over his sheep from the Church. Nevertheless they were to pay homage to the King and State for their worldly goods. The King was the Sovereign and Master and he therefore required all his subjects to respect his authority. His subjects must be loyal to him and his realm. This agreement was also to be adopted by the Emperor and the Pope who had quarrelled over the same principles.

The Theology and Philosophical teachings of Erasmus ; Calvin ; Luther; and Henry VIII's break with Rome

We begin to see a change in religious thought during the period 1485 to 1603 when the Tudors reigned over England. During the reign of Henry VII we see a change from the old medieval way to that of the modern. Nevertheless, we also see the old customs mingling with that of the new ways.

This period was the beginning of the Renaissance. There was a 'revival of learning' especially of the study of the classics. We see Greek studied with enthusiasm. New schools were founded, especially for the poor and needy. One such school was that of St. Paul's by Colet. Again we see concern regarding the education of the poor when Lady Berkeley founded a grammar school at Wotton-under-Edge in Gloucestershire. In Exeter a free grammar school was founded under the guidance of the Bishop of Exeter. The Rev. James Salter, who wrote a number of religious books was a master their in 1684. He was Vicar of St. Mary's Church, in St. Marychurch, Torquay (during this period it was called 'Tormohun) when a grammar school was founded in 1713. The invention of Printing formed a new approach to learning and it made education more accessible. The arts flourished especially in Italy where the Popes, Nicholas V and Leo X and Julius II gave artists the opportunities to exhibit their art. Bramante, Raphael, and Michelangelo did much work for the Popes in Rome where we can admire their brilliant masterpieces today.

The forerunners of the Reformation, who were referred too as 'Dissenters' or 'Protestants' (they who protested against the established Church) were Erasmus; Luther; Calvin; and an extremist by the name of Zwingle.

Erasmus was born in 1467 and he became an orphan at a very young age. He was taken under the wing of a Benedictine Order. He later became a Monk but unfortunately he left his monastery when he became a young man. He became a scholar and critic and he eventually studied in Paris. He completed his scholastic years at Oxford. Erasmus travelled extensively in Germany and Italy. Luther and Calvin were to become Protestant dissenters from the Catholic Church. Erasmus wrote "In Praise of Folly". In his treatise he is critical of the scholastic methods of the Monks. In 1516 he published a new version of the Greek Testament and compiled a Latin version. This criticism of the Church was received with mixed feelings throughout Europe.

Thomas Moore (1485-1535) was also a reformer and worked with Colet and Erasmus at Oxford for reform of the Religious Communities. They were known as the "Oxford Reformers". While many saw that the reform of the Church was necessary in this period of decadence, we see also that the Popes of the period were seeking some form of reform themselves, but they sought it within the Church. This was a slow process that the Reformers could not accept. They wanted to see the reforms taking shape quickly. However, reforms within the Church were eventually to take place but some centuries later in the form of Vatican II in 1972.

Oxford was the breeding ground for reform and it was not surprising that the Salters together with many other sincere religious thinkers would themselves become Dissenters. Thomas Moore wished for reform of the Papacy. He studied the "New Learning" and he was to write Utopia in 1526 to show the evils of the day, especially the sufferings of the poor. He wished and prayed for an ideal country with no war, no poverty, no luxury, no State Religion. He believed that labour should be shared and that all people should be happy in their work. He worked with the King and he was ready to accept Henry VIII divorce and his remarriage. The Pope would have eventually agreed to this but he would not be pushed into a decision to please a King. And after the fall of Wolsey in 1530, Moore became Chancellor. However, he remained faithful to Catholic doctrine, as did Henry VIII. It was not long before, Moore was to fall out of favour with Henry who wanted all his subjects to accept the Act of Supremacy in 1535. This was when Henry parted company with the Papacy and the Church in Rome. Moore refused to accept this new Act and as a result he was beheaded. Oxford University was a prominent place for the new thinkers. Erasmus and many of the new thinkers also taught at Cambridge University. The Salter family are seen in later generations to take up this new approach to Religion.

Luther was a monk in Germany. He left his monastery in 1508. He disagreed with the practice of Indulgences and he refused the order of the Pope to be silent. He went on to attack the doctrines of the Church. He was condemned as a heretic at the Diet of Worms in 1521. As a result a number of German princes adopted his thoughts concerning his doctrines and they became Protestants.

However, there were some extreme reformers in Switzerland and France. One of these was that of Zwingle of Switzerland. He set up his new Church at Geneva and he preached 'Predestination' and the election by 'Grace'. He had formed his Church on democratic lines and it was to be governed by elders or presbyters (hence the Presbyterian congregation). He believed that his ministers had the power to consecrate others without the authority of the Church. He did not believe in Bishops or other ranks within his Church – all were to be equal. But some more equal than others!

The three foreign Protestant Churches were Lutheran, Zwinglian, and Calvinist – they all denied the power of the Pope. They denied the role of Bishops and they denied the doctrines of the Catholic (Universal Church). They believed that services should be conducted in the native tongue of the Country and not in Latin that was the Universal language at that time in history. The Catholic Church has since 1972 adopted this teaching. The Protestants based their doctrine on the right of each man to study and interpret the Bible as they wished and not to be governed by doctrines handed down from Jesus teachings.

It should be understood that the reasons for the reformation lay in the corrupt nature of the times. The barons sought to increase their territorial jurisdiction and wealth either by force or through an alliance of marriage. This was the same with the Royal household. The same could be said for the Religious houses. The Abbots of Monasteries and some Bishops were often from the nobility. The Monasteries were becoming very wealthy. They possessed much land and they wanted more. The Monarchs began to fear the growing strength and power of the Monasteries. As a result there was much persecution against those who did not believe in their policies. Henry VIII saw in the Religious establishments too much wealth and influence. He decided to quell their growth in wealth and property by the dissolution of the Monasteries.

In later years there grew up much discontent. In many respects the poor were to suffer as a consequence. There were discontent within the Religious Establishments. There were those who devoted themselves to charity especially by endeavouring to help the poor by almsgiving and those who only sought gain and influence for themselves that was contrary to the Christian teachings. It became necessary for change. Leo X was not given time for reform of the Church. There were those who spoke out against the established Church and who did not try to influence change where it was needed most, within the Church. Inevitably schism was the outcome.

In the U.K. during the period of change in religious thought there were two main factions in conflict and they were the Parliamentarians and the Monarchy. We may place these two factions into the two major factions of Religion. The Puritans were basically Parliamentarians, who were in favour of elected government and change; whilst on the other side were the Anglicans, the High Church of England, who were supporters of the Monarchy. With reference to Charles I this meant absolute power to the King. King Charles was determined to achieve absolute authority over Parliament. He sought the financial aid of Parliament for the war against Scotland. He therefore summoned a new Parliament on the 3rd November 1640 that became known as the Long Parliament. It consisted of 128 Parliamentarians and only seventy- five Royalists. It became inevitable that conflict between the Crown and Parliament would result in civil wars. Charles I lost the conflict and on the 30th January 1649 he was executed.

In the middle of 1645 the 'Long Parliament' decreed that a Directory for Public Worship should replace the Book of Common Prayer in the Churches. Every incumbent was ordered to read this Directory on the first Sunday of its reception. There was a fine of £5 for the first offence for not complying with the dictates of Parliament and a £10 fine for the second and imprisonment for the third offence. This Directory was Presbyterian in principle. Under the Royalists many sympathisers of

Presbyterianism principles were relieved of their parochial duties and their livelihood by the taking away of their assets. The Presbyterian Parliamentarians retaliated by reinstating them to their parishes where it was believed that the Clergy were becoming rich and in some respects worldly or even irreligious.

An example of these feuds is seen in that of the Rev. Hugh Robinson, D.D. who was considered lacking in his religious fervour and therefore replaced from his parish in Dursley. He was arrested and it is said that he was made to ride backwards on his horse to Gloucester. While he was in Gloucester prison, Robinson was soon to show repentance for past ways. Gloucester gaol was dirty and in very poor condition. Robinson soon accepted change and he was to accept the 'Covenant' and in 1646 he published 'The Peoples' Plea' fully vindicating the Power and Proceedings of Parliament – the Presbyterian puritanical enforcement of their ideals. As a result he was given a parish in Hampshire. He died on the 30th March 1655 and he was buried in Saint Giles-in-the- Fields, London where some of the Salters are buried.

Joseph Woodward was to take up the vacancy at Dursley Parish Church. He was a tanner's son from Upper Cam. The Woodwards were to become related to the Salters. One of the younger Salters was to take the surname of Woodward as the middle name. This was the custom up until the beginning of the 20th century. A child would be given the second Christian name of his mothers' maiden name. When he was still a young man he was appointed Master of Lady Katherine Berkeleys' Free Grammar School in Wotton-under-Edge. It has been stated that he was amiable and obliging, but far from serious in his conduct and spirit. He was the companion of ungodly and dissolute men and he lived without God in the world. However, he was seen later to leave his old companions and associates with that of the Puritans. During this period Thomas and Giles Salter were Clothiers by trade were also seen to be pious and good practicing Christians. Woodward eventually abandoned the Latin for English in the teaching of prayer and Christianity. As Master of the School he introduced the singing of psalms and the reading of scripture among other pious exercises. When he was twenty-three he went to Oxford and gained a B.A. and later a M.A. degree. By the time he was 30 years of age he became ordained. His first sermon at Upper Cam Parish Church was taken from Acts IV v.20. As a consequence of his moral preaching he was appointed Parish Priest of Dursley.

However, to the general populous he was not so welcome due to his piety and forthright teaching. His son had referred to the people of Dursley as 'Drunken Durslians'. He re-arranged his Church on lines of Presbyterianism (Puritanism). He would offend some by refusing some members of the congregation Communion until they amended their ways. There were those who would suspend their offerings because of his strict adherence to morality. He was probably the first to introduce a Sunday - school in the area.

HENRY VIII and the final break with Rome

Henry VIII was a staunch Catholic until his death in 1547. He was never opposed to Catholic doctrine, but he was opposed to the authority of the Papacy. He believed, as did his predecessors that the Kings authority should be supreme within his own Kingdom. He did not approve of outside (foreign) influences. He was against the attacks on the Church as was seen in Germany. He wrote against Luther in his youth and Moore and Colet agreed with the King. He wanted a divorce from Katherine in order to marry Anne Boleyn, of whom he had fallen in love and he believed that she would provide him with a son and a male heir to the throne. Pope Clement VII was hesitant in annulling his marriage and as a result Henry was swift to act. He appealed to the English Universities, and he finally appealed to the Court of the Archbishops who were to declare his marriage null and void. Cranmer, who was then Archbishop of Canterbury, had publicly declared the marriage void and he gave his blessing to the marriage of Anne Boleyn. The Pope immediately responded by declaring that Cranmers' annulment was invalid. Thus the break with Rome was complete when Henry declared himself the Head of the Church in England by the Act of Supremacy in 1534. However, he was to re-affirm Catholic doctrine in the absence of Papal authority in order to uphold the Church against heresy.

Edward, the only son of Henry by Jane Seymour, sympathized with the Protestant cause. However, he was to die young. Mary who was Henry VIII's daughter by Catherine of Aragon became Queen in opposition to Northumberland who wanted the crown to go to Lady Jane Grey. Mary wanted England to be once more united to the Papacy in Rome. England was to remain Protestant and the following years were to see much persecution by both Protestants and Catholics.

The ruthless conflict between Christians was to divide the Church. Some believed that an Established Church would be a support for the Monarchy and would create stability. Lawlessness was of great proportions especially in large towns. The authorities endeavoured to punish offenders by punishment of death. Archbishop Secker wrote in 1738 "In this we cannot be mistaken, that an open and professed disregard to religion is become, through a variety of unhappy courses, the distinguishing character of the present age. This evil has already brought in such dissoluteness and contempt of principle in the higher part of the world, and such profligate intemperance and fearlessness of committing crimes in the lower, as must, if this torrent of impropriety stop not, become absolutely fatal."

A sketch of Cornwall that indicates the Parish connections with the family of Courtenay, Buller, Parker, Fathers and Salter

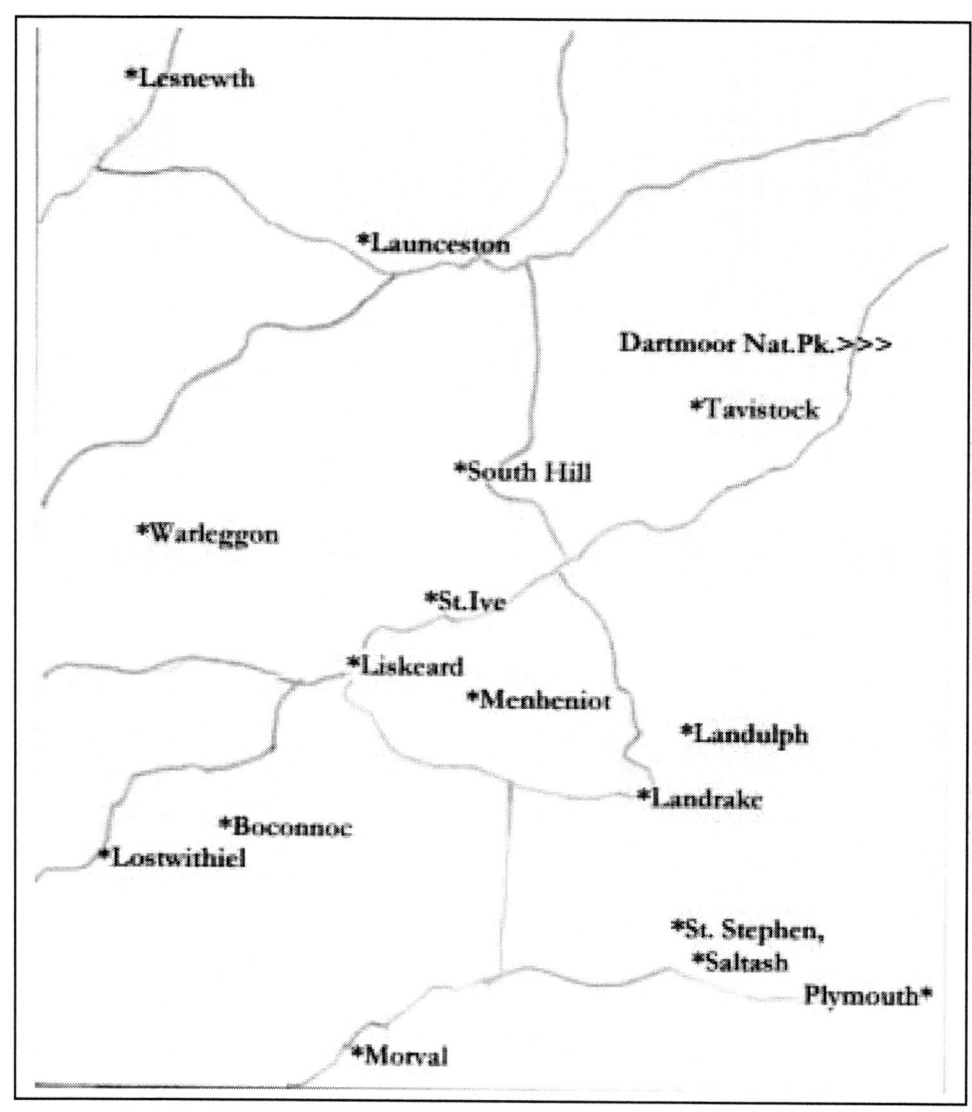

Chapter Four

·····························

Religious Links with Devon & Gloucestershire

After James II had fled England in 1690 there arose once again toleration for Non-conformity in England. It was during the reign of Mary, the daughter of James II, and her husband, King William of Orange, that an Act was passed that all non-conformists must register their Meeting Houses of prayer. Some of these non-conformists were either Quakers or Presbyterians. And it was later that we were to see the establishment of the Calvinistic Methodists and Baptists Chapels and Tabernacles. These new religious denominations began to appear all over the Country especially in the districts of Uley, Cam, Dursley, Wotton-under-Edge and Kingswood. However, there were no visible Roman Catholics at this time, but their presence was felt, especially in the open discussion between a Roman Catholic Priest and a non-conformist Minister in Stroud. The Stroud Newspaper gives a full account of this open- air discourse and a copy of these articles may be seen in the Stroud Library, Gloucestershire.

The Quakers & the Salter connections in various counties

Quakers were strict with regard to their membership. They were a source of worry to the authorities in that they would refuse to pay tithes; remove their hats in 'Steeple houses' or before magistrates and in any way compromise their beliefs. They would rather go to prison, as indeed did a Deborah Harding, a Quaker from the Dursley district. She was sent to Gloucester gaol for her beliefs. Another Quaker was George Salter, the son of a Nobleman, who was imprisoned in the Fleet prison for refusing to pay tithes.

The Quakers were forbidden to marry in the Established Church of England, which was contrary to the Law of the land whereby all marriages were to take place within the confines of the Church of England in order for them to be legal. In the mid nineteenth century the Law was changed in order to allow marriages within other Church denominations as long as the Registrar of the particular district was present to witness and grant a Certificate of marriage. This applies to marriages of the present period.

It may be noted here that William Salter, Barrister-at-Law who had mortgaged the properties of Richkings and Denham Court, was the author of 'Conversations with a Quaker' and published by Pennington in 1660. He was born in 1634 and he married Susan Vanebrug. He was buried at Iver on the 23rd September 1664. They had issue.

A great deal of persecution became the lot of the Quakers. Thomas Atkins and his wife Mary were questioned on their faith and beliefs when Bishop Nicholson visited Dursley on the 16th September 1662. Thomas was a Chandler or dealer in candles, oil, soap etc., in Dursley. Both Thomas and Mary had come to Dursley from Ross-on-Wye in Herefordshire.

Bishop Nicholson sent two Constables to arrest Thomas and Mary Atkins. They were taken to the Bishop for questioning, as follows-

Bishop – You must be conformable to the laws of the nation.

Thomas Atkins – I am conformable to the law of God.

Bishop – But I will make you conformable to the law of the nation too.

Thomas Atkins – I am made by the hand and power of the Lord God already, and I hope that neither you nor no man shall ever make me conformable to that which I know to be a sin against God.

Bishop – You are a very stubborn fellow, but I will make you submit or else I will send you back from whence you came.

Thomas Atkins – I am not stubborn, as thou thinkest; I am a man that feareth God, and I fear not what man can do unto me.

Bishop – I will make you bow, or I will make you fast enough.

Thomas Atkins – My hope is in the Lord, and thou shalt never make me bow to that which I know to be sin against the God of my life, and if thou shouldst be permitted to tear this Body to pieces, yet I fear not. I desire thee to show me that Scripture, where thou canst prove, that any true Christian, that lived in the eternal fear of God, ever persecuted any man for conscience sake; or that any of the Saints of God ever threatened any as thou dost me; if you canst, show it.

Bishop – Those whom you call Saints would persecute more than any man, if they had the power in their hands.

Thomas Atkins – Thou canst not make that appear, neither by Scripture, nor present example of those that live in the same life.

Thomas Atkins and his wife Mary were allowed on this occasion to return home.

George Whitefield, a Calvinistic/Methodist Preacher who travelled extensively was a prominent figure in the West Counties. In 1743 he was granted permission to preach in the Chapel, Castle Hill, Northampton, the benefice of which was that of the Rev. Phillip Doddridge. At this time it was thought that the Established Church of England, the Anglicans and Non-conformists persuasion would join in worship within one Church, but this was, alas, not to be.

George Whitefield was born at the Bell Inn, Southgate Street, in Gloucester in December 1714. We are told that he was a mischievous boy, and not adverse to petty stealing and at times found swearing. On numerous occasions he would enter a Dissenting Meeting House of the Rev. Thomas Cole and shout the words, "Old Cole, Old Cole, Old Cole" and he would immediately run out for fear of being caught by the Church members. However, before he became 18 years of age he began to attend regular daily services and festivals of the Anglican Church. His parents sent him to Oxford University as a 'Servitor'. A Servitor was a student who received free tuition in return for giving his services to other students. He did this for three years. In about 1733 he met and became influenced by Charles and John Wesley. However, the seeds of non-conformist of Oxford had their origins some decades before when Erasmus, Colet and Thomas Moore were students at Oxford.

During the 18th century Religious Societies which were to be known as Methodists and later Calvinistic- Methodists or Congregationalists were to be called by those who disapproved of their methods of teaching Christianity as 'Scoffers, Bible Moths, Bible Bigots, Godly or Holy Club Members'. Whitefield was soon to be accepted in the Methodists fold and he himself was to form his own Methodist Society.

These Societies were strict over religious observance and generous in their work for the poor and the needy. Whitefield later wrote; "O', with joy – joy unspeakable – even joy that was full of and big with glory, was my soul filled, when the weight of sin went off, and an abiding sense of the pardoning love of God, and a full assurance of faith, broke in upon my disconsolate soul".

Religious fervour in Gloucestershire was growing stronger and many private families were to apply for a licence so that these enthusiastic preachers could conduct a service for the praise and glory of God through prayers and hymns. Throughout the generations, the Salter families were noted for their devotedness to Christianity. Some were to become Priests, Deacons, and the extended family would take some active part within the parish community. They were also noted for their musical endeavours to sing and some would play a musical instrument, especially that of the piano or organ.

Perhaps this is why some moved to the land of song where music and religion was a very strong part of community living. We see Meeting Houses licensed all over Gloucestershire and in and around the Forest of Dean especially in Coleford where the Salters were to become Tailors and Preachers.

George Whitefield and the Wesleys were to frequently visit Somerset and Devon. The Salter family showed much hospitality to George Whitefield and the Wesleys during their visits to Saint Marychurch. It is not surprising that in later generations the Salter's were to become Baptist; Calvinistic-Methodists (Congregationalists) Preachers and Deacons. Although my ancestor the Rev. James Salter of Devon had studied at

Oxford he was there a few decades prior to that of Whitefield and Wesley. Nevertheless during his years at Oxford the seeds of non-conformity had already begun but this new religious thought did not influence him neither did it influence his son the Rev. James Salter junior. They remained loyal to Crown and Church of England as may be seen in their writings. The Rev. James Salter was to succeed his father in 1718 as Rector of St. Mary Church in St. Marychurch Torquay. He wrote "An Exposition or Practical Treatise on the Church Catechism of the Church of England" that was printed in London in 1753.

The Rev. James Salter the elder was born in the mid 1600. He matriculated at Oxford from Magdalene College on the 24th July 1668. He eventually left the University without a degree and he returned to Exeter in Devon. From records at Exeter R.O. we learn from the Ordination Papers of 1672-1674 that the incumbent of St. Stephen in Exeter had requested that he become his curate. It is also stated that he received testimonials from the incumbents of Menheniot, Bradoc, Liskeard, South Hill and St. Ive (and pronounced as Eve) in Cornwall as to his suitability for Priesthood. It is stated that he became curate of the later.

He was ordained as Deacon on the 17th July 1672. He was later ordained as Priest on the 4th June 1674. In that same year he became Vicar of Lostwithiel in Cornwall. He also has mention as serving the parish of Lesnewth during 1678/9. It is recorded however that he was priest of Lostwithiel between 1674 and 1684. At the end of 1684 he left this parish and he was appointed as Master of the Free Grammar School in Exeter. On the 4th September 1688 he was appointed Vicar of Saint Mary Church, St. Marychurch, Tormohun (now Torquay) in Devon. He remained there until his death in March 1718 when his son James succeeded him as Vicar. His son was Vicar from 1718 to 1767 when he died. They both were buried in the Chancel of the Church with other members of the family including that of the Bartlett family.

The Saint Sampson Church and the Baptismal Font used by the Rev. James Salter in South Hill, Cornwall

*The Saint Ive parish Church is situated about four miles from South Hill
and a few miles from Liskeard in Cornwall*

The Interior of Saint Ive parish Church in Cornwall

Saint Bartholomew Parish Church in Lostwithiel

The Rev. James Salter Senior Married Katherine Fathers, The Daughter Of The Rev. John Fathers of St. Stephens of Saltash in Cornwall. The marriage date is not known but it would have been about 1675/6. They had three sons namely John who was baptized at Lostwithiel on the 25th January 1679. Joseph was baptized at Lostwithiel on the 6th December 1681. He died at Lostwithiel and he was buried on the 30th December 1683. Also born of Rev. James and Katherine Salter were Katherine who was born about 1676 in Cornwall (The relevant pages for the Parish records from 1674 to 1678 are missing). She married Trustrem Langdon of Landhederik on the 21st August 1698 at St. Marychurch – Ann was born 1684/5 and she was baptized at Saint Lawrence Parish Church in Exeter on the 6th September 1685. She married John Mayo of Combeinteignhead in Devon - Elizabeth was born in 1686 and baptized at Saint Lawrence Parish Church in Exeter on the 10th April 1687. She married Daniel Lewes of Teighmouth in Devon on the 21st January 1713 – Eliza Maria was born about 1688 and she was baptized at St. Lawrence Parish Church in Exeter on the 18th April 1689 and she died young. The other three children were born and baptized in St. Marychurch in Devon, namely Mary, the twin of Martha, who was baptized on the 15th November 1690. Mary married Nicholas Wilking of Teighnmouth on the 27th December 1720. Martha remained single during this period. James was baptized on the 8th January 1695 at St. Marychurch. He studied for Holy Orders at New Inn Hall, Oxford where he obtained a B.A. He married Mary Adams of Totness at Upton Pyne on the 30th July 1728. They had one daughter Mary who was baptized on the 13th January 1729. She married Jacob Bartlett of West Hill House, St. Marychurch in Devon on the 6th February 1758. Jacob was baptised on the 22nd June 1732 and he died and he was buried on the 23rd June 1808. The Bartlett's had a wall plaque installed in the Church in remembrance to the family dead. However this was destroyed in 1943 when war-planes bombed the Church, killing the school children and teacher while they waited for the Vicar to arrive for a service. When the Church was re-built a side Chapel was erected in honour of our Lady, the Virgin Mary and in remembrance of the deceased teacher and children of the parish. Unfortunately, the Bartlett and Salter families have since been forgotten in the Church, except for documents in Exeter Record Office and the British Library. No doubt that in the future this may be rectified.

During the first beginnings of St. Marys Church there had been a number of disasters. The first was when the original Church was being built. The builders were proposing to build the Church on a lower level that is now the Teighnmouth Road. They started to build the Church only to find that the next morning the stones that had been laid were in a heap on the ground. Three attempts were made to build this Church, but on each attempt the same thing occurred. The Priest, at that time, decided to celebrate a Solemn Mass and to pray in order to ascertain the Will of God. It has been said that a voice was heard to say; "If St. Mary's Church build ye will, ye must build it on the hill". This was interpreted as God's Will, so they built the Church on the Hill where it was seen from miles around and especially as beacon for the mariner.

The second disaster struck in 1713 when a fire devastated the building. This happened during the incumbency of the Rev. James Salter, Senior. However, the Church was repaired under the guidance of the Salters. In later years, however, in the 19th century the Church was neglected and it was much in need of repair. The last disaster was the bombing raid during the 2nd World War. Both St. Marychurch and Exeter were badly hit, causing extensive damage. Exeter was to lose much of its records and Wills. However, a copy of Katherine's will may be seen at the Public Record Office, Kew; the family Archives and the Exeter Library.

St Mary Church South Porch and Priest Room

If the Salter's would have anticipated the forthcoming disaster during the war years, resulting in the death of the school children, then they would, I have know doubt, been deeply grieved by their loss. The Salter's were in charge of the first Grammar School that was established for the poor children of the parish in 1713 in the same year as the fire. Both father and son were concerned for the spiritual needs and pastoral needs of the parishioners and their children as may be seen in their writings. They were the authors of a number of religious texts and these texts may be seen in the British Library and the Davis Library in Caroline University, Chapel Hill, in America.

**A sketch of the Salter Family Arms of Devon,
as stated by William Bartlett.
These Arms consist of an Agent, a Cross-Flory
between 4 Mullets and a pierced Sable.**
*(As seen in the 'Memorials of Lostwithiel, by F. M. Hext, 1891, page 119
and as stated by William Bartlett)*

A list of the Writings of the Rev. James Salter, senior & junior between 1690 and 1767

1. "Triumph of the Holy Jesus"; a Divine Poem of the Life, Death, and Resurrection of Our Saviour by J. Salter, Senior, published in London AD 1692. A copy of this book is held at the British Library – Shelf-mark. 1077.1.3(2). There is also a microfilm copy in the U.S.A. by UMI "Early English Books, 1641-1700 Reel No.1027 (first item).

2. "Caliope's Cabinet Opened", wherein gentlemen may be informed how to adorn themselves for funerals, feastings, and other heroic meetings" SVO London 1665 by J. Salter Senior. A copy of this book is held at the British Library – Shelf-mark 605.a.10. There is also a microfilm copy in the U.S.A. by UMI "Early English Books, 1641-1700 Reel No.801 (14th item).

3. "Compendium Graecie Gramuect Catechism" SVO London. (Not listed – a record of this work is in the family archives and it is referred too by Rev. Mozeley Bartlett, a priest of Saint Michaels Mount, Cornwall and a descendent of the Salters).

4. "Sermons on The Earthquake at Lisbon, and Others" by J. Salter (Vicar) (Not listed but a record of this work is in the family archives as above).

5. "Exposition or Practical Treatise on the Church Catechism" by J. Salter (Vicar) Junior SVO Exeter 1753. A copy of this book is held at the British Library Shelf-mark 3505.bb.23. There is also a microfilm copy in the U.S.A. by UMI "The Eighteenth Century" Reel No.6099 (20th item).

6. "Prayers, &c." by J. Salter, Junior (Not listed but a record of this work is in the family Archives as above).

7. "The Pious and Well-Disposed Christian" by J. Salter, Junior (Exeter 1765 246 pp.). It was completed two years before his death in 1767. It appears that there is only one copy in existence and that this was held at Exeter Library at their Shelf-mark sB/EXE/242.8/CLA but it has since been lost.

Sketch of Saint Mary Church from Saxon times to the present day, 2002, by Godfrey Hebdon, son of Henry Hebdon, who was Secretary and Church Warden during the rebuilding of the Church after the 2nd World War 1939-45

The Saxon Church

The Norman Church

The Medieval Church

The Church in the early 19th Century

The Church on May 30th 1943

The Church today

Items 1 to 6 of the listed texts of the Salters writings have mention in a Supplement to the Torquay Directory, dated 7th November 1866. The title of this Article is 'St. Mary Church, the parish of St. Marychurch, Torquay, Devon'. It goes on to report in full the last lecture on the History of the Parish of St. Marychurch by the Rev. Prebendary Barnes. He mentions in a talk to the Working Men's Improvement Society, that the first school in 1714 would have been under the care of the Rev. James Salter. And he further states that James Salter Senior was Vicar from 1688 to 1718 and that his descendants is represented by Mr. Salter Bartlett and family and that they held land there in 1866. He also quotes a letter that was written by Rev. Mozeley Bartlett, the Chaplin Priest of St. Michael Mount in Cornwall.

The letter showed the address as 21, Southern hay, Exeter and is dated the 22nd May 1866. *A copy of this letter may be seen in the discourse as above mentioned and attached at the end of the book by the Rev. BARNES. The letter was sent to the Torquay Directory and South Devon Journal Offices and is dated 22nd May 1866.*

The following is a letter from the Rev. MOYSEY BARTLETT *that refers*

to the writings of the SALTER'S of CORNWALL & DEVON

"Dear Sir,

As my mother's family (the Salters) were formerly the Vicars of St. Mary's, I enclose a list of their works, and I should be glad if you found any of them to see them. They are in the British Museum.

Triumph of the Holy Jesus; a Divine Poem of the Life, Death, and Resurrection of our Saviour by J. Salter 4to, London AD 1692.

Calliope's Cabinet Opened; wherein gentlemen may be informed how to adorn themselves for funerals, feastings, and other heroic meetings. SVO, London 1665.

Compendium Gracie Gramuect Catechism, SVO London.

Sermons on the Earthquake at Lisbon, and others by J.S. (Vicar).

Exposition; or Practical Treatise on the Church Catechism by J. Salter, Vicar, Svo Exeter 1753.

Prayers, &c. by J. Salter.

> *I am, dear Sir, yours faithfully,*
> *MOYSEY BARTLETT*
> *Chaplin Priest of St. Michaels Mount, Cornwall.*

In his book the Rev. BARNES speaks of JOHN WESLEY and WHITEFIELD. "John Wesley was born in 1703 and died in 1791. Whitefield was born in 1714 and died in 1770. Both these remarkable men visited this parish (referring to St. Marychurch), and Mr. OCTAVIAN BLEWETT has stated in a book written in 1832 that they both did 'frequently'. St. Marychurch and Barton were to see much of these eminent preachers. They were important neighbourhoods for a revival of Christianity."

The letter showed the address as 21, Southern hay, Exeter and is dated the 22nd May 1866. A copy of this letter may be seen in the discourse as above mentioned and attached at the end of the book by the Rev. Barnes. The letter was sent to the Torquay Directory and South Devon Journal Offices and is dated 22nd May 1866.

The following is a letter from the Rev. Moseley Bartlett that refers to the writings of the Salter's of Cornwall & Devon
And was printed at the Torquay Directory and South Devon Journal offices and was published at No. 10 The Strand in Torquay, Devon

Dear Sir,

As my mother's family (the Salters) were formerly the Vicars of St. Mary's, I enclose a list of their works, and I should be glad if you found any of them to see them. They are in the British Museum.

Triumph of the Holy Jesus; a Divine Poem of the Life, Death, and Resurrection of our Saviour by J. Salter 4to, London AD 1692.

Calliope's Cabinet Opened; wherein gentlemen may be informed how to adorn themselves for funerals, feastings, and other heroic meetings. SVO, London 1665.

Compendium Gracie Gramuect Catechism, SVO London.

Sermons on the Earthquake at Lisbon, and others by J.S. (Vicar).

Exposition; or Practical Treatise on the Church Catechism by J. Salter, Vicar, Svo Exeter 1753.

Prayers, &c. by J. Salter.

I am, dear Sir, yours faithfully,

Moseley Bartlett
Chaplin Priest of St. Michaels Mount, Cornwall.

In his book the Rev. Barnes speaks of John Wesley and Whitefield. "John Wesley was born in 1703 and died in 1791. Whitefield was born in 1714 and died in 1770. Both these remarkable men visited this parish (referring to St. Marychurch), and Mr. Octavian Blewett has stated in a book written in 1832 that they both did 'frequently'. St. Marychurch and Barton were to see much of these eminent preachers. They were important neighbourhoods for a revival of Christianity."

Rev. James Salter junior was concerned that the practice of Christian worship was in decline. It needed revival by enthusiastic preachers. Thus he wrote 'An Exposition on the Church Catechism'. I now continue the quote from the book by Barnes. "They were the first parishes that contributed to the spread of their teachings in the West; here, through the kindness of Mr. Lear (the Church Warden) a large silver coin on which is engraved the name of one of their ardent supporters, Mrs. Backhouse, with the date 1778, and the engraving of an angel with a trumpet. Whitefield on his visits to St. Marychurch sojourned with his friends the Sheppard's (who were also cousins to the Salters and Bartletts) and is said to have preached in the open air in a meadow at Combe Pafford". "And here – though I am not in addressing you as a member or as friends of our Working Mans Society, touch on any topics of religious controversy, I express my own wish, in which I may trust that all join, that whatever there was of true spirituality and earnestness in the teaching of these noble-minded and devoted men may not be lost to us.... I shall be thankful, if what I have said contributes to the reverential respect for history."

Pictures of the stonework and Old Chancel of Saint Mary Church

The church ruins were moved from the church site and rebuilt as a boundary wall of 'Berrington House', Trumlands Road, St. Marychurch, Torquay, Devon.

The second picture shows the remains of the 'Old Chancel' within Berrington grounds

Some of the Salter's were in the mid-eighteenth century to move from Devon into Somerset, Wiltshire and Gloucestershire and the Christian upbringing was to follow them and where so ever they should travel.

The Church of Saint Mary the Virgin
in the Parish of Saint-Marychurch
The Rev. James Salter, senior – Vicar from 1688 to 1718
The Rev. James Salter, junior – Vicar from 1718 to 1767

The Interior of Saint Mary the Virgin Church

Pedigree of Family of Bartlett of St. Mary Church, co. Devon.

William Bartlett* of St. Mary Church, previously of Marldon, co. Devon.=Mary Bickford (first-cousin), daughter of Jacob Bickford, married at Marldon 1 April 1724. Bur. at St. Mary Church 17 Dec. 1766.
Bur. 24 April 1768 at St. Mary Church. Will proved at Exeter 21 June 1768.

William Bickford Bartlett=for second wife, Elizabeth of Tor-Mohun, co. Devon. Daughter of the parish of Bapt. 8 Feb. 1740 at St. Mary St. Saviour's, Dartmouth, Church. Bur. 2 Feb. 1813 at widow, at Tor-Mohun St. Mary Church, aged 73. Church 13 June 1801.

Mary Bartlett.=Solomon Hele Baptised at of Diptford, St. Mary at St. Mary Church Church 16 Dec. 1726. 14 Aug. 1766.‡

Agnes Bartlett. Bapt. at St. Mary Church 1728. Bur. there 21 Nov. 1728.

Elizabeth Bartlett.‡ Baptised at St. Mary Church 24 Jan. 1726. Bur. there 20 March 1728.†

---

1 w., Mary, only child and heiress of Rev. James=Jacob Bartlett of West Hill House, St.=2 w., Mary Cocking. Mar. Salter, Vicar of St. Mary Church. Baptised at St. Mary Church, gentleman. Baptised at St. Mary Church 19 Oct. Mary Church 13 Jan. 1729. Mar. there 6 Feb. St. Mary Church 22 June 1732. Bur. 1716. Bur. there 7 July 1768. Buried there 23 June 1791. there 23 June 1808. 1809.
[N.B.—All their children baptised at St. Mary Church.]

Jacob Bickford Bartlett (Clerk), Queen's College, Oxford.=Anne Christiana Emily of Aller, (B.A. 5 April 1780.) Bapt. 28 Dec. 1758. Curate of Abbots-Kerswell. Abbots-Kerswell, co. Devon, 1781—1790. Married there Bur. there 23 Feb. 6 Feb. 1784. Died 17 Jan. 1803, aged 44. Buried in old 1842, aged 80. chancel of St. Mary Church.

John Adams Bartlett, Attorney-at-Law, of Midlife Hill, St. Mary Church. Bapt. 18 June 1761. Died unmar. 6 June 1838, aged 72. Bur. at St. Mary Church.

A.

---

* Younger brother of Thomas Bartlett of Marldon, who died in 1749, and who was father of John Bartlett of Teignmouth, mentioned p. 8 infra. Described in marriage certificate as of Marldon, while his wife is described as of St. Mary Church.
† Solomon Hele was born in 1720, and had issue Jacob Bickford Hele, Esq., of Stert in the parish of Diptford, co. Devon, born in 1768 (see Risdon's 'Survey of Devon,' p. 384, 1811 ed.), also four daughters, Susannah, Agnes, Nancy, and Peggy, all named in the will of William Bartlett their grandfather. He died in 1810.
‡ William Bartlett had also another daughter, named Grace, who married a Mr. Jackson, and who was a devisee under her father's will.

The Will of Katherine (nee Fathers) Salter the wife of Rev. James Salter of Saint Mary's Church, Tormohun (Torquay), Devon

This is an extract from the Will dated 18th October 1721 and it was proved by her son The Rev. James Salter, junior (1679 to 1767) on the 20th February 1753. Katherine's husband, The Rev. James Salter senior and the Vicar of the parish Church of Saint Mary until departing this life to be with his maker in March 1718.

Witnesses were Mary Langmead, William Waymouth and William Dunn.

The Will reads –
To my daughter Martha Salter I bequeath 20 pounds.
To my son John Salter one featherbed in his own house and one tester bedstead in my chamber in the said house also a silver dish and silver spoon.
To my daughter Ann Mayo, wife of John Mayo in Combeinteignhead, 10 pounds, also one gold ring, a silver spoon and one Damask Board Cloth.
I give unto my daughter Elizabeth Lewes, wife of Daniel Lewes of Teignmouth ten pounds, one gold ring and one Damask Board Cloth.
I give unto my daughter Mary Wilking, wife of Nicholas Wilking of Teignmouth one pair of Bed Sheets.
I give unto my daughter Martha Salter one Bed and Bedding, and my wedding ring and silver spoon and all the rest of my table Linen.
I give unto my granddaughter Katherine Langdon all the rest of my household or ten pounds as my executor shall think fit to pay 10 pounds or let her to have the said goods.
Whereas I have a legacy of fifty pounds given to me and is now due to me and when payable I give unto my son James Salter for to Buy a Silver Tankard.
I give unto my son John Salter twenty shillings for to buy a gold ring.
I give unto my daughter Katherine Langdon twenty shillings.
I give unto my daughter Ann Mayo four pounds.
I give unto my daughter Elizabeth Lewes four pounds.
I give unto my daughter Mary Wilking ten pounds.
I give unto my daughter Martha Salter twenty pounds and I do hereby give unto my Trustee and well beloved son James Salter the sole and absolute power of the said twenty pounds to be managed until she is married.
I have an orchard and land in Tormohun of two lives in it...I bequeath all my right title and interest herein and there unto my loving son John Salter for and during the lives. I give unto my loving son James the rest of my residue and personal effects.

Signed and witnessed as the last Will and Testament of Katherine Salter.

Chapter Five

*Some of the Salter Family move from Devon
to other parts of the United Kingdom*

After the death of Queen Anne in 1714 – she had hoped that the Church of England would once again be united with Rome – the Anglican Church of England and the Dissenting Chapels were to proceed in following their own particular path and in their method of preaching. This may be seen in their approach to the educating of the young. As a result and because they, the Dissenters were denied entry to Universities, they established their own Colleges.

An early convert of George Whitefield was that of the Countess of Huntingdon. She became a widow in 1746 and she was then a prominent supporter of the 'Evangelical Revival'. This was mainly among the upper class of society. Her home was at Donnington Park. She died there in 1791. The records of her work with the Calvinistic Methodists may be seen in the 'Countess of Huntingdon's Connection'. In 1770 George Whitefield went to America to preach and it was there that he died in 1770.

A number of the Independent Ministers were educated and trained in the Countess of Huntingdon's own College at Trevecca, near Brecon in South Wales. This College of the Countess was founded in August 1768. The supply of Anglican Ministers had become scarce and her Chapels needed Ministers in order to conduct Services and the spiritual needs of those under her care. The Rodborough Connection had a similar experience by becoming independent. They would, however, remain in close association with other independent Churches. The Ministers chosen in Rodborough around 1778 and in Dursley about 1795 were trained in the Countess of Huntingdon's own College. It is possible that Charles Salter was also trained at the Countess of Huntingdon's College in South Wales in order to assist him in his lay-ministerial functions as well as his trade as a Baker.

A picture of Selina the Countess of Huntingdon

Charles Salter, who has had a brief mention was born in 1780 of devote Christian parents. He became a baker/grocer by trade and he was to follow his ancestors as a lay-preacher in and around Gloucestershire. Firstly, he married Ruth Derrett at the Church of St.Phillip and Jacob in Bristol on the 20th January 1800. They had issue. Secondly, he married Charlotte Peglar at St. Martin Church in North Nibley, Gloucestershire on the 29th November 1825 were they had issue. They are buried in a vault at Rowland Hills Tabernacle Cemetery, Wotton-under-Edge together with other members of the Salter family. (Isaac Salter his brother is also buried there). In order to identify the graves, there are iron-railings that surround the vault.

Diocesan records from 1724 prove that there were numerous houses that had been registered for religious worship in Blakeney and Mitcheldean in the Forest of Dean; Avening, Horsley, Painswick, Minchinhampton and Wotton-under-Edge in the Cotswolds vale. The Rev. Thomas Cole could have visited some of these towns during his ministry. He started his Ministry at Abergavenny, in South Wales in 1703 and he moved to Gloucester in 1718.

Joseph Twemlow of Cam had also contributed to the religious revival within the County of Gloucestershire. We have recorded that the Rev. Thomas Cole visited Avening, Cam, Dursley, Uley and Nympsfield. He preached his last sermon at Nympsfield and he died soon after on the 5th August 1742. A young man aged 11 years walked from Uley to Nymsfield to listen to his last sermon. The mother of this young boy, Mrs. Wilkins, had previously registered her home for religious meetings. Cole had visited this Meeting House on numerous occasions. During the 1770's a number of these eminent preachers of the Methodists Ministry were to die. It therefore became necessary for the young men within the community to continue the practice of Itinerant Preaching. This method of preaching helped to bind together the Societies within the region.

It may be of interest to the reader that during this period much artistic talent had been born. Composers of music were achieving prominence in the arts. Operatic achievements were attained. The Arts were once again to flourish. Explorers were to seek new adventures across the seas. Printing became accessible and the Gloucester Journal and the Salisbury Gazette were founded in 1772. Reading was to become the norm for all classes of society especially in the educating of the young.

It became necessary for Parishes to share Ministers due to the shortage of Preachers. Although Curates received stipends from each of the Parishes they were to serve some were poorly paid. There were few Curates that were actually capable and some lacked the necessary education. On the other hand some Parishes were poor and it became necessary for a wealthier Parish to support another. Dursley was one of these Parishes that helped to support its neighbours. It also became necessary to encourage Lay-Itinerate Preachers to fill the gap of absent Ministry.

Richard Tipping Salter and his brother Charles Salter were to follow in their ancestral footsteps. Charles became a deacon of the Baptist Church in Coleford, while his brother Richard became a Lay-Itinerate Preacher in and around the Forest of Dean. They both were trading as drapers and tailors in Coleford. Richard's great-great-grandson Keith Davies had entered the Rosminians whilst Charles's great great granddaughter, Tyann married the Rev. Peter Leonard of Llandow, Cowbridge, in South Wales. Tyann and Peter are directing people in the course of Retreats at their home and Retreat House/Vicarage in South Wales. Their children, Oliver and Beatrice have also been involved in charitable works. Oliver, worked for the Right Hand Trust – a Christian Mission Organisation – at its Headquarters in Llanfair Caereinion in Mid-Wales. He later went to work for 'Cross links' in London where he met Jo (Joanna Hewitt) and they married on the 19th August 2000. Jo had been secretary to the Bishop of Northern Namibia. They are both working as missionaries, and are now living in South Wales.

From left –Rev. Peter, Tyann, Oliver & Jo, Beatrice Leonard & friend

A picture of Richard Tipping Salter

Born 5th July 1814 at Kingswood, Wotton-under-Edge Glos.
Died 25th November 1891 in Cheltenham Glos.

Richard Tipping Salter, the son of Jacob & Mary (nee Trull) Salter was born 5th July 1814 at Kingswood near Wotton-under-Edge Wiltshire (Kingswood is now in Gloucestershire since 1844). He married firstly Harriet Jones, the daughter of George (a Carpenter) & Eleanor Jones and she were born on 6th October 1814. They married at Abenhall Parish Church in the Forest of Dean, Gloucestershire on 29th May 1837. They lived at the Poolway in Coleford where they had issue. Harriet died in 1858 and Richard Tipping Salter died on the 25th November 1891 at Bath Parade in Cheltenham Gloucestershire. He married secondly Ann Morris, the Organist at the Baptist Church. They married on the 2nd March 1861.

Ann died and was buried in Coleford Cemetery on 16th March 1884 at the age of 84.

BAPTISTS OF COLEFORD
XIX.
RICHARD TIPPING SALTER.
BY MR. CHARLES SALTER.

The subject of this brief sketch was the son of Christian parents and staunch supporters of the Baptist Denomination. He was born at Wotton-under-Edge, the scene of the labours of the famous Rowland Hill, in the year 1814. Brought up in a Christian home, and amidst good influences, he responded early in life to the call of Jesus Christ, and was baptised by Mr. Watts, the Pastor of the Baptist Church at Wotton, and received into membership. He was apprenticed to the Tailoring, and after serving his time came to Coleford about the year 1835. Here he married a Miss Jones, by whom his family, now living, was born. Some time after her death he married Miss Ann Morris, aunt of Mr. Ben Morris. She was an active Teacher in our Sunday School for many years. Tipping Salter was a strong believer in prayer, both public and private. He had family worship in the house, a custom which all christian people will do well to follow, and which when neglected, is not only a loss to the home but to the Christian Church. After dinner every day he withdrew himself for a time of quiet communion with his God. As we learn't his life was strong and healthy, being nourished by the secret springs from the fountain of the Most High. He was a local preacher, and rendered service to the congregations meeting at Parkend, Redbrook, Lydah, Symond's Yat, and several other places as opportunity offered. He was also a member of our Choir, from the time of his coming to Coleford till he left. In June, 1884, he removed to Cheltenham and attended Salem Baptist Church, under the Pastorate of the Rev. R. G. Fairbairn, B.A., where he remained till his death, which took place November 25th, 1891, at the age of 77.

MISSIONARY MEETING.

A most successful meeting in connection with the Young People's Missionary Sewing Society, was held in the Schoolroom on Thursday, October 12th, when the Rev. F. G. Harrison, of Uley, who laboured for some time on the Congo, gave a very interesting account of his work there. After the address, which was listened to with evident pleasure by all present, the meeting resolved itself in a social gathering, a musical programme having been arranged. The Action Song, entitled "Busy Little Housemaids," being the most attractive feature, the little housemaids performing their work with much energy and exactness. The work done by the Society during the year had been placed in a prominent position in the room, so that any friends interested in this branch of Mission work might see what our young people are doing for it. The work consists of 12 overalls, 16 shirts, and 12 jumpers, the last named being Miss Whitehead's contribution. The whole

will be sent to Mrs. J. R. M. Stephens, Wathen, Congo. The treasurer's report, which was read during the evening, is appended:—

TREASURER'S REPORT. 1899—1900.				EXPENDITURE.			
	£	s.	d.		£	s.	d.
Balance in hand		10	8	Hire of Dolls, &c., to London		16	0
Collections at open Meeting, 1899	1	3	6	Carriage and Duty on same to India		9	2
Refreshments sold at open Meeting, 1899		11	11	One bad for Freres, &c., for the Congo		1	0
Donations sent by friends unable to be present		0	0	Miss		0	0
Subscribed by Members							
Whole pieces sold				Balance in hand			
					£2	16	0

Generations — of Mrs Chas Salter.

The Salters

I REFER to your 'Puzzle picture' of the Salter family of Coleford.

It may be worthy of note that Charles Salter, a master tailor and draper, moved to Coleford in 1852 from Kingswood near Wotton-under-Edge. He married Sophia Howell, the postmaster's daughter.

They first had a shop at 17 and 10 St John Street and acquired premises in Market Place and Newland Street. By the way,

Charles's elder brother, Richard Tipping Salter, had already moved to Coleford in 1837 and he had established a tailoring and drapery business in the Poolway.

I have noticed on a number of occasions that Charles Salter has been confused with his nephew William Salter. William Salter was apprenticed to his uncle Charles at the age of 14 and finished his apprenticeship in Bristol, where he married. William returned to Coleford in about 1874 with his wife, Eliza (née

Furney) Salter and started a business at 1, Boxbush Road where Brian Raymond now owns the shop premises.

By the way, I am about to finish compiling a book on the chronicles of the Salter Family and I hope to have it published some time in January 2005. The second book that I hope to complete in the early part of 2005 will be entitled 'The Salter Archives from 1211.' This second book will include the family trees. – **Keith I.F. Davies, Moreton-on-Lugg, Hereford.**

Charles Salter born Kingswood near Wotton-under-Edge Wiltshire on 24th June 1824. He married Sophia Howell the daughter of George Howell a Postmaster at Coleford Baptist Church on 14th February 1852. He became a Master-tailor, as did his brother Richard Tipping Salter and a Deacon of the Baptist Church. They had issue. Sophia (sometimes known as Sarah) died at Coleford in 1914 at the age of 84. Charles died on the 12th December 1921 at the age of 97.

Another Minister of Religion that bears the name Salter was the Rev. William Augustus Salter. He was born on the 22nd September 1812 and he later became a Baptist Minister. He was educated at Totteridge by Dr. Wood and Mr. Thorowgood and he studied at the University College in London, after which he spent two years in his father's Counting House in the city of London. He was the youngest son of a pious family, and he was from earliest childhood the subject of religious convictions. The Rev. Dr. Steane baptised him in 1833 and he was called to the Ministry and entered Stepney College under the presidency of the Rev. Dr. W.H. Murch, in 1833. Among his fellow-students were his life-long friends, the Revs. C.M. Birrell, F. Tucker, B.A., and his brother-in-law, the Rev. Dr. Angus. He became the Pastor of the Baptist Church in Henrietta Street, Brunswick Square. He married the second daughter of Mr. W.B.Gurney of Denmark-Hill. He died on the 29th July 1878 and he was interned at Warwick Cemetery on Saturday, 3rd August, and the following day the Rev. Dr. Angus preached the funeral sermon from 1 Thess.v.10. He lived his life to the full as a pious and learned Preacher.

His great-great granddaughter, Isabel Henniger resides in Canada. She became a University teacher.

It has been suggested that the family tradition and Religious upbringing was a great influence for the young of Gloucestershire and we can see this in the Salter families. Although it must be noted that prior to the 19th century the changes on the continent had influenced the woollen manufacturers by way of Religious reforms as we have mentioned previously. They had come to resent the tyranny of some of those within the Established Church who would cruelly enforce their teachings upon others by force and imprisonment if they thought necessary. This cruelty can be shared equally between the Roman and Non-conformist Churches throughout Europe.

Non-conformists were usually of the middle classes. The Established Church of England was to see traders being influenced by the Missionaries from abroad especially from Holland and Germany where the Oxford Dons, Calvin and Erasmus had originated. The import of wine and the export of wool were prevalent between the Continent and the U.K. The Salters were involved in the import of wine from Flanders and the export of wool. Trade was usually done through agents in London and the agency was known as the 'Blackwall Factors'. The Salters were also connected to the East India Company that was founded by a Salter from the Shrewsbury branch of the family. Some children of the poor began to take up apprenticeships. And when they were qualified would enter the middle classes. The poor remained with the Established Church where they were helped in their education. However, other Protestant Churches began to open schools for the poor. These new schools were seen to convert their pupils to their particular Theology. They were to become independent to the Established Church.

Uley and Wotton-under-Edge had a strong non-conformists influence during the early part of the 18th century. This was to be nurtured by the Rev. John Thomas of Cam and as a result the Whitecourt Union Chapel was erected in 1793.

The Rev. Joseph Twemlow was Minister at Cam Meeting House from the time he was ordained on the 7th May 1707. His congregation increased to 800 by 1715 and he was well liked. They would come as far a field as Berkeley and Uley in which to hear his sermons. At this time the Rev. Thomas Cole was an incumbent in Gloucester. He was an Itinerant Preacher and when visiting Cam he sought the help of Twemlow to evangelise the district to the South of Gloucester. He was a reformer in many ways and the two preachers got on well.

There were many benefactors from the various businesses around Cam and elsewhere. One such benefactor was Josiah Sheppard, a Cloth Factor of Blackwall Hall in London. It was a Clearing House for the Country's Wool and Textile Trade. Other benefactors were those of the Salter families. The Rev. William Augustus Salter's father worked at the London Clearing House and he was generous in helping the Baptist Church. They were prosperous Merchants and traded in Wine and Cheese as did their ancestors in the 17th century."

The non-conformists meetings in Cam can be traced back to 1647 when Joseph Woodward became Rector of Dursley. However Cam Meeting House was founded in 1703 in the same year as the Independent Meeting House at Wotton-under-Edge that was situated opposite the Old Town Mill that is now part of the Catholic Church. Just around the corner in School Road was the Grammar School. It has now been converted into a block of flats. The Army Cadets occupied a site within the grounds of the School that is now partly derelict. This site was the Old Town Baptist Meeting House. When the Grammar School was renovated to accommodate a block of flats a vault was discovered with the remains of two young persons. We know from family Archives that Richard Tipping Trull was buried there in his grandfathers' grave at the young age of 13 months. When the renovation work began the remains of the graves were reburied elsewhere.

Richard's parents were John and Anne (nee Tipping) Trull. They are buried in the Chapel Yard at Uley that was named the Whitecourt Union Chapel of Uley. Their first son, John died at an early age of 19 and he was the first to be buried at the Whitecourt Union Chapel. He died on the 19th June 1793. John and Anne Trull were married on the 6th June 1772 at St.Martins Church, North Nibley in Gloucestershire. The family had moved from Cam to Uley in 1707 when they became members of the Baptist Church. The Baptists Meeting House was founded in 1717. During this period and up until the 19th century the Quakers and Baptist were to form a strict code of morality associated with the membership of each individual congregation. The Quakers would not allow mixed marriages even though they were Christian. In order to be in communion with their particular sect they had to adhere to the rules laid down by their leaders. However, the Baptists were more tolerant in their relationship with other Christian religious persuasion. They did in fact allow mixed marriages.

In 1673 Lydia Purnell gave a Pewter Plate to be used by the Presbyterians as a Communion Plate. This Plate is still in existence today. And in the following generation a Chapel was built in the year 1702 on a piece of land, given for this purpose by William Hicks and wife Mary, a clothier of Cam. It was known as 'Woolpens'.

This pewter plate was given to the Presbyterians of Cam in Gloucestershire to be used as a communion plate by Lydia Purnell in 1673

Photograph reproduced with the kind permission of David Evans - Author of "As Mad As a Hatter".

The Pedigree of the Trull Family

James Trull married Mary – marriage date unknown, but was probably about 1697. They had issue namely:

1. Abraham born 1703 at Cam, near Dursley, Gloucestershire;
2. John born 1704 at Cam;
3. Abigail born 1706 at Cam;
4. James born 1708 Uley – the family had moved to Uley from Cam in 1707 and during this period they became Baptists (Chapel);
5. Nicholas born 1711 at Uley;
6. Daniel born 1719 at Uley;

James Trull married and he had issue namely:

John, the son of James, was born 1747 at Wotton-under-Edge. He died at Kingswood, near Wotton-under-Edge on the 1st August 1802. He is buried at the Chapel Yard at Uley with his son John who was the first to be buried there in 1793. He married Anne Tipping who was born in 1746 and the daughter of Richard Tipping. Richard was born in 1703 and he married Ann Ponten. He died in 1774 and he is buried in the Old Baptist Meeting House. Ann (nee Ponten) died in 1779. Anne the wife of John Trull died at the age of 77 on the 6th May 1823.

John and Anne (nee Tipping) had issue namely:

1. John was born 20th December 1774 at Uley, Gloucestershire. He died on the 19th June 1793 and he was interned at the Chapel Yard, Uley. He was the first to be interned there when the Chapel was built in 1793;
2. Anne was born 2nd July 1776;
3. Joseph was born 15th May 1778. He married Elizabeth Seaborn on the 15th March 1801 at Coaley. Elizabeth was born 6th January 1776 and she died in 1854. They had the following children,
    (a) James was born 1st January 1802. He married and had issue;
    (b) Sarah was born 12th March 1804;
    (c) John was born April 1806;
    (d) Ann was born in 1812;
    (e) Elizabeth Seaborn Trull – birth date unknown.
4. Mary was born 14th March 1780. She died on the 19th February 1860 at Wotton-under-Edge, in Gloucestershire. She married Jacob Salter, the son of

George and Margaret (nee Axton) Salter, on the 26th December 1803 at Kingswood, Wiltshire (now the County of Gloucestershire).

5. Benjamin was born 8th August 1781. He married Elizabeth Dauncey on the 5th September 1799 at Uley in Gloucestershire. They had issue namely:

    (a) Richard was born 31st August 1800;

    (b) Martha was born 15th November 1812;

Benjamin served in the Military from 1801 to 1811. They later moved to Bristol.

6. Martha Trull was born 8th August 1784 at Uley;

7. Richard Tipping Trull was born 3rd November 1787 and he died on the 1st June 1788. He was buried with his Grandfather (Richard Tipping) at the Old Baptist Meeting House, in the Old Town of Wotton-under-Edge.

The Old Baptist Meeting House was converted into a School House and it is now a Block of Flats and Scout Meeting House. A grave was found during renovation work and the bodies removed elsewhere. This was probably the Vault of the Trull family.

A Short Obituary of Two Members of the Trull Family

Richard Tipping Trull was born on the 3rd November 1787. He died on the 1st. June 1788 at the early age of 7 months. Mr. Simmons preached at his internment and chose as his text Lamentations 3, "It is good for a man to bear the yoke in his youth". His funeral text was, "It is the Lord, let him do what seemeth him good". He was buried in his grandfather's grave in the Baptist Meeting House at Wotton-under-Edge, in Gloucestershire.

John Trull, the honoured father of the above children died 1st August 1802. He was interned with his son John in the Chapel Yard at Uley. Mr. Sabine gave out a hymn, and he read the scriptures and prayer. Mr. Simmons gave an oration from the pulpit. Mr. Sabine gave a short oration at the side of the grave, and Mr. Simmons concluded with a prayer. Anne (nee Tipping) Trull the beloved wife of John Trull died on the 6th May 1823 at the age 77. She is interned with her husband and son at the Chapel Yard at Uley.

The Whitecourt Chapel at Uley in Gloucestershire

A Research carried out by my cousin Henry Trull of Buckinghamshire

The information received from Wayne Trull of Tasmania in Australia refers to his great-great-grandfather Richard Trull who was born in 1829 in the district of Bristol. It would appear that Richard is the son of Richard Trull who was born in Uley on the 31 August 1800. His grandfather would have been Benjamin who was born 8th August 1781 and Elizabeth (nee Dauncey) Trull and they were married at Uley in Gloucestershire on the 5th September 1799.

Richard Trull who was born 1829 married Ellen Ford on the 5th September 1853 and they arrived in Tasmania aboard the "Raleigh" in 1855 together with their infant son also named Richard. He was baptized as Samuel Richard Trull on the 26th November 1854. They were 'assisted immigrants'. The "Raleigh" departed Southampton in late 1854. Richard Senior was described in the passenger list as a GLS farm labourer. Further research confirmed that their roots were of Uley in Gloucestershire.

Most of Richard's descendants live in Northern Tasmania with a small number living in the state of Victoria.

Benjamin Trull served in the Military from 1801 to 1811. They later moved to Bristol.

Henry Trull is the descendent of Joseph Trull who was the brother of Benjamin Trull. Joseph was born 15th May 1778 and he married Elizabeth Seaborn in 1801 at Coaley

The following is an extract from research carried out by Henry Trull of some of the origins of the name Trull.

"Most occurrences of Trull in England occur in 2 clusters, South-West and South-East. The Western side, which is where my own interest lies, is clustered in and around Gloucestershire and Bristol. The assumption I have made is that when they left the land in Gloucestershire as part of the major migrations from country to town in the eighteenth nineteenth centuries, Bristol was the largest city in the vicinity at the time. The Eastern Trulls about whom I know nothing seem to be in and around Kent, about which I can comment no further.

The South-West is the part that sticks into the Atlantic, comprising from South-West to North-East of the Counties of Cornwall, Devon, and Somerset, up to the city of Bristol and then Gloucestershire to the north and then Herefordshire which forms the border with Wales. Bristol was one of the largest ports in England in the 18th century and it became very rich when it was engaged in the triangular trade, from England to West Africa (iron goods and pots), to the Indies and the Americas (Slaves), and back to England (sugar and cotton). However, as the ships grew larger, the restricted depth of the Avon caused Bristol to go into decline as a port and Liverpool and Southampton superseded it.

There is a village in Somerset called Trull, which has become a suburb of the town of Taunton. I once visited the village and talked to the local vicar (often a useful source for local history). He informed me that Trull was a corruption of Trendle, and the local 'big cheeses' had originally been called Trendle. By the way the Church has some very fine stocks in the churchyard. Another item of information is that one of the leading agitators in the Cornwall (Kernow) independence movement is a Fred Trull."

Further research carried out by Henry Trull revealed that there is a small village near Uley that is called Trull. However, this is not shown on a Map due to the fact that it is a hamlet rather than a village. It was established that at the time of the land enclosures in 1730 there is a 'Trull-house' that is situated on the edge of Cherington parish that is three parishes from Uley. The estate of Trull Farm was created from a large former open field and common land allocated to Lord Ducie for his Hazleton estate in 1730. The name was changed to 'Down Farm' in 1791.

It is recorded that a James Trull bought some land in Herefordshire in 1483, the year Richard III was killed at Bosworth-Field the last battle of the Wars of the Roses. It has also been recorded that he bought and sold land in 1487 that was adjacent to the previous plot of land.

There is record of a James Trull of Wortley and a Nicholas Trull of Uley who paid hearth tax in 1662 and also a Richard and Samuel Trull who made an oath of allegiance to William III in 1695.

***"Trull House" situated between Rodmarton and Tetbury
and about four miles from Uley in Gloucestershire***

Chapter Six

·······················

The Cloth & Woollen industries in the West Counties and other imported commodities to the Port of Bristol

During the 15th and 16th centuries we see the Woollen and the Hating Industries expanding. Not only was trade brisk in the United Kingdom but export was good too.

Landowners saw the profits to be made in sheep farming. If they did not farm the land themselves they would let their land to farmers for agricultural or livestock production. It became a known fact that clothiers sought after the best quality fleece, and later we see some clothiers rearing sheep themselves in order to procure the best wool for the Home Counties and overseas markets.

The Sheppard's of Somerset and Devon were producing wool via their own herds of sheep. However this was only done in a small way and they still purchased wool from other sheep farmers. The sheep that were best for good quality fine cloths were regarded as 'Marino Sheep'. They were purchased either in Cornwall or South Wales.

In the later part of Henry VII's reign he bettered his commercial policy in conjunction with his Parliament. He wished to increase and improve the woollen export trade. His chance came in 1506 when Phillip of Burgundy became ship wrecked on the English Coastline. Henry seized on the opportunity and forced Phillips hand to sign a commercial treaty that gave England such favourable terms for the export of wool. The Flemish referred to the agreement as the 'Malus Intercursus'. In addition the old Navigation Acts that were passed in the reigns of Richard 11 and Edward 1V were re-enforced by Henry. The Acts ruled that English ships would be used to take goods from England to a foreign port, and therefore, woollen cloth was to be exported via English ships.

It was also agreed that wine from Gascony was to be carried in English ships. The Salters of Shropshire were also connected with the wine trade about this period. Sir Nicholas of the Court, Buckinghamshire was a prosperous London Merchant and a founder of the Hon. East India Company. He paid enormous sums to James 1 and he held the monopoly of French wines. He paid from £16,000 to £21,000 per annum. He was granted a licence to conduct a weekly market at Enfield in 1616.

Besides London and Southampton, Bristol in Somerset was also a thriving Port. In 1497 we see Bristol Merchants shipping merchandise to the new continent of Americas, via the Cape of Good Hope. Under the guidance of the Venetian leaders, two English explores, namely John and Sebastian Cabot reach the shores of America. John Saltern and his brother William were Bristol Merchants during the mid 16th century. The spelling of Salter was also spelt as Salterne as was noted in Chapter One with reference to the various spellings.

Extract of will of JOHN SALTER a Merchant of Bristol (16th c.)

"Saltern, John of Bristol a Merchant was dated 4th October 1577. Reference C.M.Cell.8/36. P.C.C.30 Arundell.

Proved 6th August 1580 by procurator of John Salterne, power reserved to William Salterne.

I will that when God shall send home the Swallow of Bristol, wherein I now go forth for Mallorca & Sesilia that my books may be very diligently perused & accounts given up unto those for whom this voyage I am Factor.

Alice the servant of Mris. Preise to have paid her at Michaelmas next £4 that I owe her as by account thereof in my Book may appear in folio 120.

To John S. son of my brother Richard S. £10 at age of 20.

To the Universities of Oxford & Cambridge to the relief of poor scholars £10.

To the poor of Bristol £5 & of Bideford £3.

To my godson Etheldred son of Richard Edwards 40/- towards his maintenance at school.

To my brother Thomas S. all my apparel.

Residue to my sisters Anne & Phillippe S. equally at marriage. And in the meantime my brothers Richard & Thomas Salter to have the said monies in their custody. My most dear Father John S. of Bideford & my loving brother William Salter of Bristol, a Merchant to be my exors.

A view of mine Estate of what I am due to have. Item, mine Adventure now forth in the Swallow of Bristol for Mallorsa & Sesilia £190. Mine adventure for the Matheras & Tercera jointly with Mr. Aldworthe in the Gabriel & Jhus of Bristol £50. Mine adventure resting in custody of John Radman £20. Andrew Cottrell oweth me £8.8.4. My brother Richard S. oweth me £8.6.8d. Myles Dekonson oweth me £10 to be paid at the recovery of the goods laden in the Valentine of Bristol, which was taken by the Frenchmen.

My brother Thomas S. oweth for percells as follows: Item that he shall receive for me of Wm. Dies £9 of Simon Aldworthe £10 & also £25 & others 17/7d - £4.2.5d. £10.3.4d. £3 & £20. (A reference to folio in his accounts in each case).

A view of what I do owe. To the use of Mr. George Smyth the elder to be paid in Mallorca £20. To Thomas S. £29 & also £15. (A reference to folio in his accounts in each case). Item £305.3 in the balance of this account besides such profits as God shall send by my ad. Adventures.

(P.C.C.30 Arundell)

The East Indian Company was founded in 1600 in order to promote trade with the East. The Company had its Head Quarters in London and it was granted a Charter by Queen Elizabeth I. The Company was to open a Depot/Factory in 1613 at Surat on the West Coast of India and then later in 1639 at Madras and in 1661 at Bombay and later in 1690 at Calcutta. It was successful in establishing Depots in India mainly due to Political influences. The Portuguese were rivals to trade. They had attempted on numerous occasions to establish a footing on Indian soil, but Captain Thomas Best of England, thus procuring the approval of an Indian Ruler of this region, defeated their ships.

The East Indian Company imported tea direct from China and it became the beverage of the elite. It would usually be served soon after dinner. John Orvington wrote an essay on the virtues of drinking Tea, entitled "The Nature and Qualities of Tea". It was consumed in the custom of the Chinese by way of a circular cup with no handles and a saucer. It would be drunk black and sometimes with sugar but no milk as is the custom today.

Towards the later part of the 17th century Coffee was introduced and imported by the East Indian Company from Jamaica and Barbados. During this period Jacob Henry Webb, the son of John (a Clothier of Stroud) and Sarah (nee Salter) Webb was baptized in 1822. The British Government sent him in the reign of Queen Victoria to the Bahamas in the West Indies, firstly as a School Inspector and later as a Government Official.

It was not long before Coffee Houses became established, as was Tea towards the later part of the 17th century. However, in contrast to Tea Premises, they were viewed as possible breeding-grounds for dissension by the Government of the time. Hans Sloane who travelled intensively had a servant called John Salter who accompanied him on many of his travels abroad. Eventually, John Salter was to open his own Coffee House in the 1690's in Chelsea and it was called Don Saltero's. His first Coffee House was in Danvers Street and then at 18 Cheyne Walk. Although there were other Coffee Houses such as in Paradise Row and the Five Bells Tavern, perhaps Don Saltero's in Chelsea proved to be the most interesting with its curios. Trophies that had been collected by John Salter on his numerous travels furnished it and visitors also added to his collections and eventually it developed into a museum. After he died his daughter continued with the Coffee House and Museum until the 1760's and at the end of the century the contents of the Museum was sold, fetching £50. It then became a Public House until being demolished in 1867. Sir Hans Sloane died in 1753 and he left his collections of antiquities to be housed in the British Museum together with items from the first and second Earls of Oxford. The British Museum was opened in 1759. Sloane had been a physician & botanist and he was the founder of the Botanical Gardens.

During the later part of the 15th century some of the Salter's had moved to Dorset, Devon and Somerset where they were to take up farming and also be in some way involved in the Textile Industries. The production of cloth and salt were the main source of productivity within the British Isles, taking up an equal share of the market; and before the dissolution of the Monasteries the monastic communities were also involved in the production of wool. The wool and cloth production by the monks can be traced back through to Saxon times and even as far back as the Bronze Age. However, land was taken away from Monasteries and then handed over to those persons who were in favour with the authorities, the government of the day and the Monarchs.

It has been said that while the Peasants (the poorer of the nation) work long hours in order to reap the harvest, the barons, the landowners reap the wealth and the Kings reap the benefits by way of taxation. The only rest for the Peasants are from the Holy days which is now called Holidays. The winter season starts from 29th September, Michaelmas to Christmas when wheat and rye are sown, and then there is Lent to Easter where barley, beans, peas, oats and vetch are planted. Summer is the result of sowing until 1st August. Then follows the harvest and the winter once again.

The rest periods throughout the year denotes the Churches festivities. In December, Christmastide, we celebrate the birth of Christ. In the spring the Lent fast begins the 40 days of Lent through to Passion Week or 'Holy week' that is followed by Easter (the Risen Christ). Another festive occasion would be celebrated on the 1st May that is known as the "May-day celebrations". It is an ancient custom depicting two events. One is the celebration of fertility where members of the district, the neighbouring parishes, would come together, usually on top of a hill to make dance around the Maypole. This would be a tall pole set on top of the hill with strands of coloured cord. The people would hold onto the ends of the cords to dance clockwise around the pole creating an interwoven thread. There is a myth that is recorded in a book called "Mythology of the British Isles" by Geoffrey Ashe in the chapter entitled "Hillside Figures". It relates to the Cerne-Abbas Giant in Dorset. It was believed that if a girl slept on the giant figure she would bear many children, and that a barren woman could be cured. The word 'Trendle' that has mention in the previous Chapter also refers to Maypole dancing which took place on a neighbouring earthwork called the Trendle. Trendle may also refer to a circle or round. Another ancient custom that is celebrated on the 1st May is where villagers from the lower regions of a particular hill would assemble in groups on top of that hill to fight for the possession of it. This could be a relic of the "Campus Martius" an ancient custom as mentioned in the New History of Gloucestershire by Samuel Rudder in 1779.

Too name but three such places where these events took place were 'May-hill' which is situated off the A40 road from Ross-on-Wye to Gloucester. May-hill may be seen from the Stroud Valley on the one side of the Severn estuary and the northern side from the Malvern-hills to Hereford and Worcester. Another such place is situated on the top of the Malvern-hills that overlooks on the one side the Severn estuary towards Stroud Valley and on the other side Hereford and Worcester and Welsh Black Mountains. The third such example is that of the Stroud Valley itself. Just outside Uley there is a hill that is an ancient Britton Burrow. This overlooks the Severn and Welsh Hills.

Another celebration was that of Rogation days when Parishioners would process around their village in order to 'beat its bounds'. During this procession the description of land (or a survey as it is called today) and the inhabitants would be duly recorded. Midsummer would also have its special festivities as on the 24th June. The season of Lamas-tide begins on the 1st August where one would celebrate the end of the wheat harvest. During these periods of festivities and up until the 20th century there was much community involvement on the special celebrated days. However, alas, we in the U.K. have since lost sight of Carnival celebrations. Instead our Continental brothers appear to be reviving the act of celebrating special occasions with enthusiasm and colour. In the old days the common folk would become as one with the gentry and celebrate such events.

Sheep, as we have considered earlier was one of the main sources of wealth in the Country. There were over six million sheep being reared in the 12th century of which 50,000 sacks of wool each year was produced. The export trade was thriving and the English wool was greatly sort on the continent because of its high quality and what was termed as good value. The main export was to Flanders where Europe's cloth weaving was based. King Henry II imposed a tithe on wool, as did other monarchs in order to finance their particular military expeditions that proved unpopular but this was extracted by force if necessary. One can imagine the wealth procured from wool and sheep when in the 12th century £70,000 was brought in by way of taxation. Even though large sums of money was placed into the Exchequers purse the landowners, and this included the Monastic communities, became very wealthy. In Salisbury alone £25,000 was obtained in 1189 in order to pay for the treaty arrangements with the King of France.

King Edward I wanted to control the wealth of the barons and gain for himself some of the wealth of the nation so as to pay his debts incurred with Italy and the Crusades. Some of the Courtenay and Salter families were involved in these crusades to the Holy Land. Edward had already incurred new statutory legislation to curb the growing wealth of the Church. William I had done the same in 1086. Edward appointed Commissioners in every County in the Kingdom to ascertain the ownership of land, livestock and chattels. The results were recorded on scrolls or documents that were presented to the King.

These scrolls are very informative to the historian. Each scroll bear the seals of juries appointed for the task and they are known as the "Ragman Rolls" because of their ragged appearance. There were in the region of hundred rolls produced within the country.

After King Edwards return from the Holy Land and Italy and his visit to his lands in Gascony he prepared for his great coronation day. This took place on the 19th August 1274. However after the death of his father, Henry III, and some twenty-one months prior to his coronation he was proclaimed the new King of England. He made provision for the celebration of his coronation and ordered that "60 oxen and cows; two swine; two fat boars; 40 bacon pigs and 3,000 capons and hens for his feast" should be prepared. In addition to these he ordered the Monasteries to provide swans; peacocks; cranes; rabbits and kids whilst the fishmongers were to supply pike, eel, salmon and lampreys for the big day. The Coronation was to be celebrated by all ranks of society, from the aristocracy to the peasants where all the population would enjoy the festivities.

Towards the latter part of the 12th century people were becoming more aware of cleanliness. Bathhouses were frequented, especially by the wealthy. These Bathhouses would not only be used for medical purposes but they would also be used for pleasure as in social meeting houses where one could bathe in warm springs, as seen to this day in Bath Spa. They would chat and enjoy some food and drink. During this period soap was being manufactured from goats tallow and beech ash and often olive oil was used for the cleansing of the skin. In addition sponges and perfumes were being used to give the body some fragrance and refreshment.

We have some idea as to how the nobility lived in style from their budget accounts. Lord Thomas de Berkeley, baron, owned estates in and around Thornbury, Sharpness, Dursley, Wotton-under-Edge and he occupied a Castle in Berkeley. Berkeley is situated near to the Severn Estuary and South of Gloucester and North of Bristol. His budget accounts during the period 1346 gives us an insight into what it would have cost for a nobleman to live in style. He would spend around £1,308, of which more than half went on household food, and a great proportion of this would be for entertaining his guests. He needed to travel around his estates and as far as London. Therefore it was necessary to procure and keep a good stock of horses in his stables. On average he would spend about 11% of his income for this purpose. Most of the money that was set aside would be spent on feed, straw for bedding, harnesses and riding tackle together with other stabling equipment. About £26 of this was spent on buying new horses and falcons for sporting. His personal clothing bill came to £142. This amounted to more than his household linen. The household linen and silver amounted to approximately £45. £21 was to be spent on wax for lighting and an equal amount would be spent on building costs. His extra expenditure amounted to £86 and this would include arms, boots, shoes and wages.

Now that we have considered briefly the cost of living and the local activities during these periods, we can now look more closely at the Industries themselves and how communities earned their incomes.

Whilst some of the Salter, Bartlett, Parker, Cole and Webb families remained in Devon, Dorset and Somerset, others moved Eastward towards Bristol, Bath, Wiltshire and as far north as Gloucestershire looking for work. Some would be involved in tin mining and although tin mining was a good source of income in Cornwall there were new sites opening up in the north of Bristol around the Frampton-Cotterell area that is situated south of Gloucestershire. There was also new ground to cover in farming in Somerset and Gloucestershire. Sheep, as we have already mentioned, was a necessity for the wool trade that flourished within Wiltshire and Gloucestershire. There were other commodities such as Flour Mills and bakeries. Dairy products were the main diet for the ordinary folk. Wine making was also very important. Tea was only imported in 1700 so the natural beverage was that of water or wine.

Cloth making was a prominent feature in the middle-ages to the early twentieth century in and around Somerset, Gloucestershire, and Wiltshire, but it is not without note that prior to watered powered Mills became an innovation the more concentrated areas for producing cloth was in South Wales and Cornwall, that is known as the West Counties. However Cloth was also produced in the Northern Counties from Shropshire to Yorkshire. We can trace wool production from the Bronze Age to that of the Roman occupation and through to Saxon times. Shropshire would acquire their wool from the Welsh Sheep Farmers across the border and they would subsequently manufacture it accordingly.

The processing of the wool into cloth would firstly be the preparation of the wool by scouring by means of warming it in a solution from the soapwort plant or perhaps in water and urine that was known as sig. Then it would have been rinsed in a running stream and then allowed to dry in the sun. When it was dried out it would have been beaten with rods in order to rid it of any burrs and dirt. The yarn making consisted of two processes. Firstly the Wool would be combed in order to lay the fibres parallel. And then needed to be spun by way of a wooden or bone spindle which would be fitted with a circular whorl at the lower end as one would see in the actions of a flywheel. Finally the yarn would be rolled into a ball.

In the 17th century there were many Clothiers in and around Somerset, Wiltshire and Gloucestershire. To name but a few there were the Sheppard, Webb, Salter, Hale and the Rossiter families. All of these families were to be linked by marriage. It may be noted that the Hale family have their roots well and truly established within the Stroud Valley and the Rossiter family in Frome, Somerset.

The Sheppard families were to become cloth manufacturers at Frome in Somerset and Uley in Gloucestershire. The Webb family were to obtain factories on the outskirts of Stroud in Gloucestershire and they had factories in Wiltshire. We can see the Webb and Salter families unite in the marriage of John Salter to Mary Webb in 1647 and again in the 19th century we wee the families joined in marriage. John, the son of Samuel Webb a clothier near Stroud married Sally who was also called Sarah after her sister who died in the year of her birth in July 1785 at Frampton-Cotterell. They married on the 30th March 1807 at Wotton-under-Edge in Gloucestershire. Another branch of the Webb family owned and occupied Ham Mills, Stroud that is now a Carpet Factory and Museum.

A Thomas Salter has mention in 1608. In the Wotton-under-Edge parish archives he is recorded as trading as a Clothier from Marston in Wiltshire. He married at Kingswood near Wotton-under-Edge on the 11th April 1631. Another member of the Salter family is recorded in the 17th century in the name of Giles Salter. And Jacob Salter, the brother-in-law of John Webb, became a Carding Engineer Dresser in the Kingswood and Wotton areas of Gloucestershire.

We find that in the 13th century Cards were being used to prepare the wool for spinning. These Cards were boards set with a uniform covering of small wires and these were held in place by projecting handles. In later years the spinning wheel was introduced and the Spinner would operate the wheel with one hand and direct the wool with the other hand. By the end of the 18th century the weavers became concerned when the hand operation of the carding was to be replaced by machinery. It was considered that the use of machinery would reduce the manual labour and as a result aggressive protests became manifest within the Cloth and Textile Industries.

The Devonshire and Somerset branch of the family were associated with sheep farming and as previously mentioned connected in some way to the Church. It would appear inevitable, therefore, that future generations should become involved in the Woollen and Cloth Industries. However, future generations would see a decline in the Industry.

It was in the latter part of the 19th century that the Salter's became tailors. This was probably due to the fact that the Cloth Industry was in decline. There was seen to be much poverty within the regions of Wiltshire and Gloucestershire. Needless to say the Salter's were engulfed in this poverty stricken area. The Clothiers were becoming bankrupt and falling like ninepins. The weavers were in fear of losing their livelihood by way of the introduction of machinery. This resulted in riots within the Industry and it was prevalent throughout Somerset, Wiltshire and Gloucestershire as well as the

Northern Counties where disputes were of a greater proportion. Some Salter's managed to survive the unrest. One such person was that of John Salter of North Nibley who was a Spinner and Clothier by trade. His son William became a tailor and moved across the Severn-estuary and into the Forest of Dean and settled in the town of Coleford. In passing William was able to write with both hands at the same time. With the right he would write as normal but with the left he would write backwards. Was this not a coincidence when we consider the Wool Spinners using both hands to perform different actions with the spinning wheel, as did William's father John?

Chapter Seven

Hatters in the West Counties

A number of Cornish, Devonshire and Dorset families had moved to South Gloucestershire, Bristol and Bath in Somerset where trade was brisk in the Felt and Hating Industries. The Felt trade was flourishing in the 18th century and Bristol became a booming export terminal and Market town.

To name but a few of the immigrants from the West Counties were the Webb, Cole, Parker, Bartlett and Salter families. However some of their relatives were already established in this part of the Country. George Cole became established in St. James Parish of Bristol and his son George became Alderman of St. James. The Webb family had established themselves in the Cloth Industries around the Stroud Valley, while the Parker, Bartlett and some of the Cole families took up agriculture and Tin Mining in and around Frampton-Coptterell and the Forest of Dean. The Salter family took up various trades as Butchers, Millers, Bakers, Victuals, Mariners and Hatters, Clothiers and in later generations as Tailors.

Frampton-Cotterell became well known for its Hating Industry. Hatters were seen to be trading in the North East of Bristol and South Gloucestershire for at least 300 years and up until the mid-nineteenth century. One of the first to actually build a factory for Hating was that of W.H. Moore & Co. Mr. Moore had established a factory just outside Frampton-Cotterell in an adjacent hamlet known as Oldland Common. However, by the end of the 18th century his factory was to close. Nevertheless, it was not long before the London firm of Christy was to establish themselves as the main Hating Manufacturers in the district.

George Salter, the author's ancestor, was born of devout Christian parents sometime in the first half of the 18th century. Although the family resided in and around Wiltshire and Gloucestershire during this period the family originated from Devon. It was a period when the Woollen and Textile Industries was experiencing good times. George had fallen in love with Margaret Axton, a girl of Draycot-Cerne who was born in 1747. She conceived and it became necessary for them to marry. They married at Little Somerford on the 21st March 1774. Witnesses to the wedding were Isaac Day and Reynolds. Their first son James was born July 1774 and he was baptized on the 10th

July 1774. It was soon after the baptism that the family moved to Frampton-Cotterell. Frampton-Cotterell is situated about 4 miles north of Bristol. George was a Miller and Baker by trade.

The family remained at Frampton-Cotterell for about 15 years before they moved to Kingswood near the town of Wotton-under-Edge. Prior to their move to Kingswood they had ten children that were born in Frampton-Cotterell. Kingswood was in the County of Wiltshire until 1844 when it became part of Gloucestershire.

Their second son Isaac was born about 1775 and he was baptized at Westerleigh Church on the 17th March 1776. Isaac was apprenticed to the Hat trade and it is most likely that he did his apprenticeship with Moore at Oldland-Common. His family lived there until the 19th century. When Isaac had completed his apprenticeship he became qualified as a Master Hatter and Journeyman. A Journeyman was a qualified person who conducted his trade from his own premises and he would carry out additional work for various Manufacturers. Christy & Company of London would eventually be one of these Manufacturers to whom he served. Christy had established their factories in Frampton-Cotterell and Rangeworthy.

Hatters on the whole were quite poor, as were the Weavers in the Cloth Industry. They were earning only 8 shillings a dozen hats and they had to supplement their income by growing their own vegetables and some kept their own chickens. Potatoes, bread and eggs were part of their essential diet. Some would have a pig as a luxury. In some circles you would be termed as 'middle-class' and quite ' well-off' if you possessed a pig in your household possessions.

Ann Fry, a Quaker, wrote in her diary of 1812 concerning the state of the Hatter in general terms. She wrote; "They labour under great anxiety. From the high price of bread they are compelled to begin upon their potatoes before the usual time and these will not carry them through the winter. The scenes of such misery plunged us into suffering". In all the villages around Frampton-Cotterell namely Winterbourne, Rangeworthy, Pucklechurch, Cadbury Heath, Oldland-Common and the Hamlet of Kingswood near Bristol and a place called 'Made for ever' that was a small hamlet were finding their economy difficult to manage. There had been a great struggle against poverty during the latter part of the 18th century and the beginning of the 19th century. The Salter's were fortunate in that they had a father who was a Miller and a Baker who could supply the family with their essential diet and necessities.

George and Margaret Salter wished for their sons to be educated. They therefore arranged that Isaac would be apprentice to a Hatter whilst Jacob was to be trained as a Carding Engineer Dresser. Proof of this may be seen in the fact that they were able to write and sign their name fluently. However, other members of the family did not achieve the same academic heights until a later generation.

The Hating Industry in Frampton-Cotterell and its neighbouring parishes was seen to be operating from at least the seventeenth century. The Hatters during this period and up to the nineteenth century were making woollen felt hats for export. As early as 1761 they were producing hats for Virginia, Georgia, Africa and the West Indies. There were at least 70 Hatters working and producing hats at Frampton-Cotterell during the early part of the 19th century. The weekly consignment of hats was shipped from Bristol docks. Bristol was the main port, other than London, for the export trade. Each ship contained approximately 30 dozen hats per cargo and probably more for the West Indies when the season came around for the sugar cane to be picked. Slave pickers needed hats for the season to protect them against extreme heat from the sun. A better quality hat was known as a 'Beaver-hat'. These would be sent to London where they went through a finishing process. These hats were then sold through an agency such as the 'London Factors'. They were also agents for the Clothiers. These hatters were paid on a commission basis of 8 shillings per dozen hats supplied.

Christy was well aware of the Hating Industries capability in the West Country. They had been in contact with the Western Hatters over many years and they had seen the potential for a factory where there may be less trouble with the unions that were causing so much concern for the Company in London.

Although the Hatters of Frampton-Cotterell had their own Felt Makers Society they were not associated with the Unions of London and they were considered that they would be better and less troublesome. They, the Felt Makers Society had their own Clubroom in Frampton-Cotterell. On a special feast day in May they would get together and walk in procession. A band would lead the procession with a person at the head carrying a 'well cocked hat' on top of a pole. They would proceed to the local Church where they would hear a sermon. After the Church Service they would go to the local Inn where they would enjoy a pint of beer and lunch. This was probably a ploughmen's lunch.

The following is a quote from the Hatters Gazette by D. Vinter; "Possibly a kettle with its sloping top which held the boiling water (to which dregs of beer was sometimes added) into which the embryo-hat was dipped, cooled and drained repeatedly until it had shrunk to half its size. The Villagers had now done their share of the work and the hats were then sent to London by stage-wagon for all the finishing processes. The loads were taken up at regular stopping places along the London Road, one of these being at the cross-roads near Keynsham Church." It may be worthy of note here that the hats did not go through the finishing process in the district of Frampton-Cotterell but the Hatters were only responsible for the Bowing, Basoning and the Planking of the hats, except for the straw hats that were intended for the Slave trade in the West Indies. These hats went to the Port of Bristol to be shipped to the West Indies.

The Founder of the Christy Company of London was Miller Christy. He was born in Scotland and he became an apprentice to his brother-in-law, William Miller, a hat maker and Burgess of Edinburgh. At the age of 20 he went to London and worked for a Master Hatter in the Strand. On 1st March 1773 he opened a Hat shop with a partner Joseph Storrs. However, this partnership ended in 1794 and the business became known as 'Christy and Company'. This may be termed the beginning of the Christy Empire.

In 1797 his eldest son Thomas became a partner, and in 1800 his second son, William Miller Christy also became a partner. When the founder, Miller Christy retired in 1804 his third son John joined the partnership. It was at this time that the brothers decided to move to premises at 35 Gracechurch Street. This became the Head Office of Christies until 1954. The Factory was at Bermondsey and therefore became known as the Bermondsey Factory. By this time Christies was flourishing and they were to obtain another Factory at Stockport near Manchester. However it was not long before the employees, together with their Unions, protested against low wages and the introduction of machinery. They eventually went on strike. These disputes concerning the introduction of machinery was also to be experienced in all areas of the Felt Industry within the U.K.

The Trade Unions were well established in London and its suburbs. Because of the problems in London it was decided to expand and look elsewhere in order to avoid any disastrous loss of trade and possible closure. Although there were many trade organizations or societies being formed in the West Country there were no Trade Union. Trade Unions were first established in the year 1831, but this was only the beginning. These Societies were militant forces sometimes forming into mobs of violence and in some cases they would burn down factories if they did not get their own way. However these militants were mainly associated with the Cloth and Woollen Industries. The Hatters, on the other hand, were Craftsmen who were not necessarily committed to any particular factory. Nevertheless this situation was to change when the Hatters became associated and in some cases employed directly with a Company.

By the turn of the 19th century Christies was considering opening up a Factory in the West Country and by the year 1818 the Company had made up its final decision.

In 1813 the Christie family decided to send an expedition to Frampton-Cotterell. On the 18th July 1813 the three brothers, Thomas, William and John Christie Miller (at about this time the spelling was changed from 'y' to 'ie') accompanied by six men made their way to Frampton-Cotterell in order to ascertain the possibility of establishing a Factory there. The following is a quote from their diary: "We came…with six men to make trial at this place."

Five years later and when the troubles in London were getting worse, they purchased property on the 12th November 1818 that was to become their first Factory in the district. This consisted of the Managers House with the Factory next door as depicted in the Picture:

This picture shows the Managers house and factory

At the back of the building there was a larger complex. This other building was purchased and it became the Main Factory.

This picture shows the main factory at the rear of the buildings

The gentleman seen to the left of the picture is a great grandson of Mr Skinner, a building contractor who purchased the property in 1874 after the factory was moved to Stockport. When this picture was taken he was in his 90th year.

Each Bower worked in front of a small window with a partition between each window. The tunnel-light produced from these small partitioned windows was necessary for their work.

By the 1830's the Company were proving very successful and they were soon to open another factory in the village of Rangeworthy that is situated about 8 miles from Frampton-Cotterell and this Factory was to become a subsidiary to their main Factory. About this time they had also opened a Factory at Wray in Lancashire. In 1831 their employees joined the London Union that was known as the London Fair Trade Union. The local branch was established at Winterbourne. During this period they were employing more than 120 Hatters at Frampton-Cotterell and at Rangeworthy a little over 40. The Manager at this time was that of a Mr. Luke Fowler.

Since the arrival of the Christie Company Frampton-Cotterell was prospering bringing in more people into the area looking for work. The population had risen from 1,208 in 1801 to 1,816 in 1831. Prior to 1843 Christie was making 110 dozen Hats per week at the Factory at Frampton-Cotterell alone. However, it was soon realized that their problems in London was to follow them to the West Country through the grievances brought to the forefront by the Union.

Although the Unions had only gained members in 1831 at Frampton-Cotterell they were already enrolling new members at Oldland Common as early as 1829 and probably earlier as they were the main cause of the closure of Moore's Factory. The men at Moore's Factory who did not join the London Fair Trade Union were classed as 'foul men'. Mr. Moore was forced to close his factory because of violence and the disruption of work. There were militants within the membership who preferred violence to arbitration. The Vicar of this Parish tried to make peace between the two sides but without success.

Things went comparatively smoothly for the Christie Company and by 1843 they were employing about 160 men and they were producing approximately 1,400 Hats. However, soon after 1843 trouble broke out again for the Company. London was once again in turmoil. The felt makers within the West Country went out on strike in sympathy with the London men. This was to prove disastrous for the Hatters in the districts around Frampton-Cotterell. The disputes gathered momentum. The main grievances were –
1. The workforce believed that they were under paid for the hours they worked.
2. They wanted their colleagues in Stockport to be able to join the Union – the Unions threatened strike action if they did not join and become members of the London Union.
3. The introduction of Machinery for fur cutting was not welcome as the work force feared for their jobs. A similar situation was seen in the Cloth Factories were the Weavers objected to the introduction of machinery in their Factories.

Christie's knew that they had to keep apace with this new development. They had to consider their position carefully if they were not to end up in the same predicament as that of Mr. Moore at Oldland Common. They were also faced with the added problem of competition from other Hat Manufacturers who were modernising their Factories in order to satisfy the growing demand for the modern designs of silk hats. Although they always kept abreast of new designs and they had already started to manufacture silk hats, they needed to modernise and extend their Factories. They also needed the machinery in order to improve efficiency.

As early as 1860 some of their employees were moving either to Stockport or Bermondsey. In the year of 1864 a decision had to be made as to which Factory would be modernised and expanded in order to meet the requirements of their customers. Styles were changing and improving constantly. It was essential that the Company of Christie should be in a position to compete with their major competitors. It was decided to move all their equipment to Stockport in the year 1864. They had come to this decision partly because of long drawn out strikes with their Company during the periods 1845 to 1860. It was also true to say that the workforce at Stockport were less militant. Their employees were given the opportunity to move to Stockport or to their London Factory at Bermondsey.

The reason for the move to Stockport was one of economies and efficiency rather than their problems with the Unions. Although the objections by the Unions and some of their members against the introduction of machinery for fur cutting was a defining and major factor.

I am including the following notes in the event that it may be of interest to Local and Family Historians.
1. Some of the families that moved to Stockport were the Rodman; Cryer; and Brown families.
2. One of the Hatters remaining in Frampton-Cotterell was that of Mr. Pullin who obtained his own business.
3. Rodman became a fur dealer in Stockport.
4. Julia Cryer of the machine room at Stockport retired in her late years about 1953. Her father had been the Manager of the Christie Company. Her ancestors were from Frampton-Cotterell.
5. W. Hardy became the foreman blower for the Company and his father was Mr. S. Hardy Of Frampton-Cotterell.
6. George Flower became the foreman Planker.
7. The great-grandson of S. Hardy became a foreman settler at the Stockport Factory.

After the departure in 1864 of the Christie Company from Frampton-Cotterell the main premises were occupied by the following;

1. The main Factory was first sold in 1874 to a Mr. Skinner who was a builder/contractor who was helped in the purchase of the property by Dr. Fox.

2. On the 22nd June 1876 the property was sold to H.R. Farguest & Co.

3. In 1958 Mr. H. Rogers was the occupier of this property. Mr. Rogers a travelling Showman used part of this building as a workshop for his Acts.

4. By the 1990's the premises was converted into residential Flat accommodation.

Prior to this property being converted into flats you could still see the pegs above the windows from which the bows were hung. A short distance from the Factory was the Hat Makers cottages. It is possible that Isaac Salter and his family lived near and in similar style cottage. The Planking of the hats would have been done here as the Cottages were situated near a stream. A stream or river was essential for the production of hats as in the Mill Factories for the production of Wool. They needed good clean water for their work.

In 1966 the Christie Company had merged the Felt Hat Industry into one company and it was later sold to Associated British Hat Manufacturers that was known as ABHM Ltd. John Christie-Miller of the sixth generation became the Chairman of this New Company. When Lord Cardigon bought ABHM Ltd in 1980 he changed the name back to its original name of Christie & Company and he reinstated the family trademark and logo. John Christie-Miller retired as Chairman and a Director of ABHM when Lord Cardigon took over the Company.

In the next Chapter we will consider the Unions and the Chartist Movement in and around Wotton-under-Edge and Dursley.

Chapter Eight

Unrest and the rise of the Unions & Chartist Movement

In the early part of the 18th century during the reign of Queen Ann we see a number of conflicts associated with Politics and Religion. The Jacobites wanted the Stuarts to succeed to the throne in succession to Queen Ann. Queen Ann's brother James Edward Stuart was a Catholic. The Protestant Government feared that James would re-introduce Catholicism back into England. Although Germans, the Hanover household were not a popular choice, they were staunch Protestants. After the death of Ann on the 1st August 1714 Parliament proclaimed the accession to the British throne of Prince George of Brunswich-Luneburg, the elector of Hanover and a second cousin to Queen Ann. However the Stuarts and their followers, who were known as Jacobites, tried to overturn the Act of succession by numerous revolts with the added support of Spain, a Catholic Country, but without success. This brought to an end the Stuart dynasty.

During this period there were two distinct classes of people within the United Kingdom. These were the Workers and the Gentry or Landowners. There was growing discontent among the workers. Their wages were kept low and their standard of living was mediocre. The ruling class were of the opinion that if the workers were given too much wages then they would only spend it on Gin & Ale. There were numerous unorganised riots that were soon to be quelled.

The first attempts to organise groups of workers was seen in the establishment of Friendly Societies. In 1719 we see the Shoemakers forming a Friendly Society in Newcastle-upon-Tyne. This society was to unite workers in the cause for mutual benefits.

Robert Walpole who was leader of the Whig Party and Prime Minister during the early part of the 18th century was a popular leader when he first became Prime Minister due to his repealing the Salt Tax that proved to be very unpopular. However in 1732 he reintroduced the Salt Tax much to the disgust of the poor. Another unpopular Tax on the poor was the introduction of Tax on Gin the poor mans beverage of pleasure. Another unpopular tax was the Cider Tax of 1763 that was introduced by John Stuart, the Earl of Bute in Cardiff.

On the 25th June 1753 in Taunton Somerset, women were a force to be reckoned with when price rises would prevent them from affording bread for their families. Bread was a basic diet especially that of the poor. These women were frustrated with the excessive rise in the cost of living. The Mill Manager was accused of selling their flour elsewhere in the country forcing prices for bread to rise so high that they could not afford a loaf of bread. They wanted the corn to be sold locally in order to help the local economy. However, they went to extreme lengths in order to protect their families from hunger. They prevented the corn from being transported to other parts of the Country by destroying the Mills. What they did not consider was that by so doing they were destroying the means of producing food.

Sir Robert Walpole died on the 18th March 1745 at the age of 69 after a gruelling two decades in Politics and as Prime Minister.

Jethro Tull (or Trull) devised a machine seed drill that become very popular with farmers. It replaced the haphazard system of scattering seeds. Instead it would plant seeds in a straight line at regular intervals and depths and then it would cover the seeds with earth as it went along the field. He also invented a mechanical hoe. This new technology helped to make farming more economical and productive. However some feared that it would create less manpower and that it would cause unemployment. This became the general fear in the Textile Industries when machinery would take over from manual labour to a certain extent in the end of the 18th century and the beginning of the 19th century.

In 1758 Land enclosures were introduced where Common Land was sold to Farmers. This enabled Farmers to take control of Common Land in order to increase a greater yield and profit and they were to prove much more suited for modern crops and their methods of harvesting. This however did not fair well with the poor peasants who used the Common Land for hunting or gathering firewood from common wastelands. The loss of food and firewood for their homes resulted in riots in protest against the ban on their activities. The ordinary villagers, if caught procuring off Common Land were arrested and fined. In many cases they could not afford the fine and they were either imprisoned or transported to a term of years in a foreign Country.

Another contention was seen in the Cloth Industries. In Lancashire a Carpenter from Blackburn invented the Jenny in 1765. His name was James Hargreaves and he was 35 when he invented the Jenny. His machine allowed eight threads of cloth to be spun in one movement. This was to create unrest among the Weavers, as did the invention of the Fly Shuttle. The Fly Shuttle increased the speed of the handloom and John Kay invented it in 1753. Although Weavers worked for Clothiers they actually worked from home.

Again we see that the Weavers and the Handloom Operators feared any improvements would result in un-employment. By the 10th May 1768 Hargreaves had built a number of Jennies for sale. These Jennies were becoming popular within the Textile Industries but not so with the Weavers. The Weavers feared for their livelihood and independence. Both Spinners and Weavers broke into his home and destroyed the machinery. He was not deterred and decided to take up a partnership and they moved to Nottinghamshire in 1769.

Although the Textile Industries were making good profits the poor of a community were seeing the cost of living rising and that a number of workers were threatened with loss of earnings. The rich were getting richer and the poor were getting poorer. Families had to allow their children to work in order to earn a loaf of bread. Children as young as eight were being employed as cheap labour. The price of Wheat had increased twofold and as a result families could not afford bread. This made the ordinary folk in a community to unite and protest. This resulted in riots. In Barnstable Market in Devon a protest also resulted in a riot. We have already seen that Friendly Societies were forming to protect the individual's rights to justice and in later generations we see the role of the Unions.

During the Napoleonic Wars between 1783 and 1815 and Prime Minister Pitts Government bread once again became very expensive to purchase. However there were some landowners who tried to help the poor. One particular landowner and family member was that of Jacob Bartlett of the parish of St. Marychurch in Devon. Jacob and his wife Mary (nee Salter) Bartlett were living at West Hill House. He married Mary the only daughter of Rev. James (Junior) and Mary (nee Adams) Salter. Their son James Salter-Bartlett became heir to the estate known as Ilsham-Barton Farm. This estate had been in the family for a number of generations and it extended to about 350 acres. The Bartlett family also owned a large number of scattered fields in and around the parish of St. Marychurch and also a Corn Mill. They decided to help the poor by selling corn at a cheaper rate than elsewhere.

The Bartlett family are recorded in 1475 as shown by the Manor Court Rolls. Again we see mention in a grant from the Abbot of Tore in 1520 in the names of John Bartlett, Senior and Roger Bartlett Junior.

From the middle of the 18th century and the beginning of the 19th century we see the beginning of the Industrial Revolution. As we have considered previously the rich were getting richer and the poor were getting poorer. The poorest of the poor were referred to as the Proletarian class. The Industrial Revolution saw the beginnings of Capitalism.

Capitalists believed that change was necessary to improve profits by way of the introduction of machinery into factories. However, the poor saw the introduction of machinery as a threat to their livelihood. Weavers and Spinners were working from home. They feared that they were in danger of loosing their jobs due to the introduction of machinery. As a result of this riots and in some cases violence occurred.

However, there had been numerous attempts in the past to help the poor within the U.K. Queen Elizabeth during the later part of her reign accomplished two important aspects of unemployment. She endeavoured to keep people employed and to ensure proper payment for those employed through the introduction of the Statute of Apprentices in 1563. In each district the Justices were responsible to draw up rates of pay for all categories of employment. The scale of wages would be based on the cost of living in a particular district to ensure a reasonable living standard. Districts within the realm varied.

Another concern was the state of the poor and unemployment. In 1601 Queen Elizabeth was responsible for the Poor Law Act. Each parish would be responsible for its own poor. The Justice of the Peace was to administer. A rate was levied on each household by the Church establishment. The Church authorities were responsible for the distribution of monies to the poor.

In 1600 we see a new era in commercial development. Queen Elizabeth granted charters to great trading Companies. Charters were granted to the Muscovite Company in Russia; to the East-land Company in the Baltic; to the Levant Company of the near East; and the East India Company who pioneered the "Joint Stock". The members pooled their Capital and Profits.

One of the founders of the East India Company was a John Salter of the Shrewsbury branch of the family. Selina, Countess of Huntingdon, was also responsible for free schools in Wotton-under-Edge in Gloucestershire and she would help young people to become apprentices to a particular trade or profession. In 1768 she had established a theological college for Clergy in Breconshire.

Although there were those concerned with helping the poor there were those who appeared more concerned in procuring wealth. As a result the poor and those who feared the loss of their livelihood would rebel against what they considered the prosperity of richer classes. They felt that machinery would cause much hardship amongst the proletarian class. They thought that by destroying such modern methods of production they would safeguard their standards of living. They did not see that such action was to destroy the very nature of improvements to their standard of living.

The Industrial Revolution saw the change from Agriculture to that of Factories and Machinery. The 18th and 19th centuries were to see a change of life. Some villages were to become towns. Towns and villages became industrialised. However long before the Industrial change there were workers who endeavoured to form into groups within their particular community. This was not to form into a national group of workers.

That was to come later. These groups would form a Guild. This was a local organisation, a combination of Master-craftsmen in the workforce. Some were to achieve more than others. For some the growth in commerce, the increase in wealth and capital gave rise to the birth of Capitalism. This gave rise to a national economy and power. Certain individuals, who had increased in commercial enterprise, are known as entrepreneurs. They became wealthy and not just locally but nationally. Even among the Masters of a particular trade there became a wide gap of inequality. And some became less wealthy whilst others became wealthier.

A Guild was neither an employers association nor a trade union nor a joint association. A person would begin as an apprentice and on completion of his studies would become a Guild member. It was not a matter of class distinction but rather of attaining the fruits of ones labour. However where capitalism began to show its head, it was the result of Masters showing skills in trade and commerce. They were to acquire much wealth and prosperity. But this did not mean that all would achieve equal success. Some would do better than others and this would eventually show in a class structure in later generations. Capital was no longer a local issue for town and country. It became a National economy by the rise of a few entrepreneurs.

The Guilds were formed partly for equality among men. However because of the growth in capital of some traders in commerce we see some becoming more equal than others. This was to some extent tolerated among the Guild members. As a result their strict rules were somewhat weaker than had been originally accepted. The 17th century saw the decay of the Guilds. Those who now controlled the government of the Guilds were becoming too powerful for the Journeyman who was at the threshold of his career. Some in high places within the Guild tried to curtail the size of the Guild by increasing its fees. Eventually some journeymen were forced to give way for the richer members of commerce. They had little hope of becoming Guild Masters. As a result Journeymen attempted to form their own association outside of the Guild in order to enforce better pay and conditions. The Guilds tried to suppress these movements. This may be seen, as the beginning of Trade Unionism. It would unite workers nationally.

In 1677 there were a group of workers who staged a partition in the town of Trowbridge endeavouring to persuade the Clothiers not to reduce their wages but to increase it. It was suggested that for a twelve-hour week's work an increase of 6d should be achieved. Prosperity of trade up to 1720 saw a period of tranquillity and as a result the workers were prepared to accept their plight. However it was short lived. Due to the shortage and high bread prices and limited cash flow a riot broke out in many parts of the West Country. The Government was concerned with the outbreak of riots in Trowbridge, Bradford and Frome where cloth was produced in large quantities. They feared that the Jacobite sympathisers might take advantage of the current situation. Nevertheless the weavers who were religious dissenters from the established Church blamed the clothiers for their low wages. In their hats they wore the letters K.G.W that stood for King George's Weavers. They claimed that the Clothiers used weights of 17 oz to the pound for spinning and lengthened the warps by three or four yards, and that this was the result of low wages. The Government, in order to curtail more riots introduced certain remedies by an Act of Parliament that required the Clothiers to pay the Weavers by the yard.

By 1738 there was a decline in the cloth trade that resulted in more unrest. Matthew Coulthurst, a Clothier of Melksham in Wiltshire, produced a warp to weavers at a reduced rate. This caused unrest and, as a result, a mob of weavers from Trowbridge went and destroyed the cloth in his weavers' looms. Four of the ringleaders were arrested and three of them were executed by hanging. Concerning these riots a writer who called himself 'Country Common Sense' wrote an article on the riots for the Gloucester Journal (December 1738). Part of this essay was reproduced in the Gentleman's Magazine giving the article national prominence. The writer of this article was a clergyman from Seend who owned much land in the area. Andrew, we are told gave a balanced view as may be seen in a quote from the article, "It is not fit that Masters should be suffered to oppress their Servants, force them to take Goods, in Defiance of Law, at an Exorbitant Price, nor enter into Combinations to fall their Wages, in a Free Country. Nor is it fit that Servants should be let alone to take their own Revenge on their Masters; it is, indeed, a pity they should be driven to it". He realised that the weavers had grievances but he also placed the blame, as did other writers from Trowbridge, on the Blackwell Hall Factors who sometimes kept clothiers short of money by imposing long credit.

William Temple wrote a somewhat extreme Pamphlet that was published in 1739. "The Case as it now stands between the Clothiers, Weavers, and other Manufacturers with Regard to the late riot." Temple believed that the Act of 1727 was incomplete because he believed that the Magistrates were not giving a fair and just hearing to the case of the Clothiers.

We are told that the Industrial Revolution began in earnest after the War with France that ended in 1815. However, we need to look back to the latter part of the 18th century to really observe the beginnings and what affect it had in Politics and the domestic front.

Agriculture was the first Industry to see reforms by improved methods of farming. However the new methods proved to be beneficial to the increase of productivity in both arable and the rearing of Cattle, Sheep and other livestock. The method of farming had remained the same up until the 18th century. Arable land was sown with corn for two years and the third year it was left to fallow in order to give the land time to fertilise itself. Nevertheless, by the end of the 18th century it was discovered that by growing rooted plants such as turnips, barley, a mixture of clover and some form of grasses helped the feeding of livestock on the farm and help the fertilization of the ground through manure and thus keep the soil active throughout each year. This rotating of the land was to prove a great success. Due to this method of farming it no longer became necessary to slaughter Cattle and Sheep during the winter months. Instead it gave winter feed to the farm livestock.

The Government saw the importance of this and therefore introduced a new Department that became known as the Board of Agriculture. George 111, before he became ill, became interested in these new methods of farming and introduced this type of farming at Windsor. He also wrote articles in Agricultural newspapers encouraging other farmers to follow his example.

It became necessary to obtain more land for the growing of crops so the Government introduced new legislation by way of Common Land Enclosures. This increased the productivity by the rich landowners. The smaller landowners were forced to sell their farms due to the fact that they were now unable to supplement their income by the use of common land for grazing purposes. The poorer community, who relied on obtaining firewood from common land, were now forbidden. If they were found breaking the new laws then they would be fined or if they could not pay the fine then they would be imprisoned or even transported for a number of years. The yeoman class and small farmers became labourers to the gentry or prosperous farmers. It was inevitable that some sought work in the towns where factories were being established.

The poor became restless because of unemployment and the restrictions that were placed upon them. The poor labourers found much hardship and began forming groups of workers to try to improve their state. The Government were worried concerning the revolution in France so they tried to prevent groups of workers from forming mobs that would protest against their plight. Therefore the Government introduced more legislation by way of the Combination Act.

George Salter whose ancestors came from Devon married Margaret Axton at Little-Somerford in Wiltshire on the 21st March 1774. After their first child, James, was born they moved to Frampton-Cotterell where they had another 8 children. George was a Miller/Baker by trade. Their children were educated at the local Grammar School. Isaac was born in 1775 and was baptized on the 17th March 1776, was apprenticed to W.H. Moore & Company, a hatting manufacturer whose factory was situated in a small hamlet known as Oldland-Common. However this factory was to close before the end of the 18th century due to disputes and the threat of the Textile Union that was based in London. This Union tried to persuade workers from various parts of the U.K. to become members. They were sometimes aggressive in their approach at recruiting new members. During this period there were no unions in this district. They were to establish themselves later in the 19th century when Christie and Company had established themselves in Frampton-Cotterell. By the end of the 18th century Isaac had become a Master Hatter and Journeyman. He worked from home and he would have done work for Christies. He lived at Oldham Common but after retirement he moved to live with the family in Wotton-under-Edge. He died in October 1856 and he is buried in the family grave with his brother Charles.

Charles, son of George and Margaret Salter was baptized on 5th March 1780. He followed in his father's footsteps and became a baker. He also became an Itinerant Preacher for the Congregational Chapel at Wotton-under-Edge in Gloucestershire. The members of the congregation were also associated with the Presbyterian persuasion. He died on 28th November 1856 at the age of 76 and he is buried in the Tabernacle Churchyard with his second wife Charlotte who died 10th May 1855 at the age of 66.

George and Margaret Salter's next son was Jacob Salter, the authors' third great-grandfather. He was born on 22nd February 1782 at Frampton-Cotterell and he was apprenticed to the Textile trade as a Carding Engineer Dresser. He moved with his parents and siblings to Kingswood that is situated a few miles from Wotton-under-Edge. They lived at Abbey Cottages and George Salter and John Trull, the father of Mary Trull were Miller/Bakers at Abbey Mill. Up until 1844 Kingswood was in the County of Wiltshire and after this date it became part of Gloucestershire. Jacob Salter and John Trull have mention in the Baptist Archives as being a member and Trustees of the new Baptist Church dated 16th July 1816. The building of the new Church in Rope Walk was completed in 1818. His wife Mary (nee Trull) was the granddaughter of Rev. Richard Tipping who was the founder of the original Baptist Meeting House in the Old Town, Wotton-under-Edge in 1717. Joseph Trull the grandson of Rev. Richard Tipping is also mentioned as a Church member and he is referred to as a Pig Butcher by trade.

David son of George and Margaret Salter were baptized on 24th June 1787 at Frampton-Cotterell. He became a Cloth-Finisher by trade. He married Anne Tidman on the 28th October 1813 at Wotton-under-Edge. They lived in the old part of the Town.

During the war years with France the Textile trade was good and new innovations were being developed and invented that was intended to improve output within the Textile Industries. Therefore it is possible that George and Margaret Salter decided to apprentice some of their sons to enter this profession. However there were those who opposed change for fear of the unknown. The family would have known some of the militants for the rights of the Weavers and the poorer classes within the Textile trade around Wiltshire and Gloucestershire.

The second son of Jacob and Mary Salter was John. He was born 3rd November 1804 at Abbey Cottages, Kingswood, Wiltshire and when he was old enough he was apprenticed as a Woollen-Spinner. After his apprenticeship he became a Clothier within the district of Dursley and Wotton-under-Edge. He married Elizabeth Pick of Cromhall; near Kingswood on 2nd May 1831 at The Church of Saint Mary The Virgin in Kingswood and after their marriage they lived firstly in Kingswood where their first five children were born. They later moved to Gloucester Road in North Nibley where their other children were born namely Hannah born 1845 and William born 1847. Their first son George Frederick was born in 1831 and baptized on 3rd February 1833 on the same day that his father was baptized at the Independent Chapel in Wotton-under-Edge.

The family would have known the militant Timothy Excell who became a very prominent figure and he proved to be a good orator who wanted fair treatment of the poor and a fair wage structure within the Cloth Industry. However he did not approve of the political agitators known as the Chartists Movement.

Other members of the family were John's aunt Sarah (known as Sally) who was the sister of Jacob and David Salter. Sarah married John Webb of Stroud who was a Clothier and manufacturer. He served with Nelson during the war with France and was given medals for his services. Another connection with the Cloth industry within the Stroud district of Gloucestershire was Esther Trull who married William Perrin a Clothier and manufacturer. His factory was situated a few miles from Dursley on the left hand side of the road to Uley. It is now known as Mill Farm.

There were those who welcomed the introduction of machinery while other members of the family sympathised with the militants who feared for the welfare of the journeyman. Modernised factories were to change the life of the community. There was bad feeling between the Masters and the workforce as was seen during the depressed winter of 1807 to 1808. There was unrest concerning low wages especially when some Masters wanted to lower the income of the weavers and spinners. The weavers and spinners were finding it hard to compete with the new machinery. In about 1806 the Sheppard's who had Mills in Uley in Gloucestershire and Frome in Somerset were concerned of the unrest prevailing during this period.

Their Mills were to be visited by Nemnich, the Secretary of the Hamburge Chamber of Commerce. He was warned against the mention of the introduction of machinery to the workforce for fear that a riot would ensue. Most of the workforce did not want the introduction of machinery in case it meant the loss of jobs.

The Luddites who were active mainly in Yorkshire and the North of England would threaten Mill owners against the introduction of machinery and they would go to extreme measures by burning Mills if their demands were not met. They also influenced the weavers and the Shearing Frame workers in the West Country. An example may be seen in the Mill owner William Payne who was threatened and suffered strikes in his Mill. John Lewis of Briscombe received a threatening letter that his Mills would be burned if his workers were not given a better wage.

It was later discovered that a young boy of 18 had actually sent the letter and he had signed it 'E. Ludd' believing that the authorities would blame the Luddites. However in the Gloucester Journal of 29th July 1812 the boy was sentenced for falsely subscribing a letter with menacing words and he was subsequently transported for 15 years. There were also disturbances at Kings Stanley Mill in 1819. In 1819 Edward Sheppard of Uley was also to experience disturbances at his Mills. And in 1826 there were riots and strikes in Stroud and Chalford and later rioting took place in Wotton-under-Edge. These riots have mention in Gloucester Journal dated 10th April 1826.

Timothy Excel of North Nibley mentioned earlier was often referred to as the 'king' when he formed the first trade union of weavers. An article dated 17th July 1882 in the Gloucestershire Gazette refers to 'the king' and gives an account of Gloucestershire Woollen Industry. Also in the Gloucestershire Journal dated 5th December 1825 page 3 column 3 there is an account of the riots that took place in Wotton-under-Edge and known as the 'Chipping'. It may also be noted that the Chartists Movement was prominent in Gloucestershire and various meetings took place in the 'Chipping' of Wotton-under-Edge. It is quite possible that some of the family were present at these riots and meetings but it has not been proven. Some family members however would have kept their distance from such events especially when they were associated with the manufacture and the supply of Cloth.

Chartism was more a political movement than a trade union organisation. Timothy Excel played a large part in the strike of 1825 but he was opposed to Chartism and in meetings with the weavers he presented good arguments against it. He had hoped for some reward for his efforts suppressing the movement but he did not get his desired rewards.

The magistrates in the Stroud area of Gloucestershire were very concerned regarding the agitators of the Chartists Movement. The movement appeared peaceful except for some violence that was caused by provocation. In Trowbridge there was very little damage done through the rioting in that town. In an attempt to quell riots of discontent the leaders of the Chartist Movement were imprisoned and this action did curtail some activities of the members although some activities continued until the year 1842. During this period of unrest the Chartists endeavoured to make common cause with the Tories in order to retain the Corn Laws supposing that the abolition of the Corn Laws would create lower wages. However this did not go down very well with other members of this movement in that they disapproved of the Corn Law and wished for its abolition. The Stroud Journal of 9th September 1871 referred to the leader of the Gloucestershire branch of the movement as 'mild in nature'. He disapproved of bad language and violence and believed that workers in the Cloth Industry were doing better for themselves than their masters.

Another reason for discontent was when the French wars had ceased. French Silk was now to be imported to England. This in turn sparked concern and the weavers therefore rioted. There were many out of work and when the army recruits for the War Years, were demobilized unemployment became even greater. The rise in imports and the slump in exports to the colonies made matters even worse. The wartime boom was soon followed by recession and who did the workers blame but the Government especially that of the Duke of Bedford who had negotiated peace with France.

Workers wished to improve their working conditions and they were to form what was termed as 'combinations' which was later to be known as 'trade unions' but the Government was swift to quell these movements by introducing new laws. Because of these new measures to curb groups of workers with serious legal consequences the attempts by most trades during the 18th century were short lived. The consequences for contravening these new laws resulted in 3 months gaol or two months' hard labour. In some cases where appeals were allowed they were too costly to entertain.

During the latter part of the 18th century and the beginning of the 19th century Cotton had become the largest Industry within the U.K. and export became a thriving business to Europe and the U.S. As a result Cotton workers demanded higher wages during 1808/1809. 100,000 cotton weavers in Lancashire signed a petition and sent it to the House of Commons. However Spencer Perceval, the Chancellor of the Exchequer, and a number of his colleagues believed that a minimum wage would force many small firms out of business. By 1812 bread prices rose again and the poor were to feel the pinch. It may be of interest that Gas lighting was introduced on the streets.

At the end of the war with France riots broke out once again concerning the rise in Corn prices. Mobs had rampaged across London due to Parliaments controversial Corn Law prohibiting foreign imports until the home price had reached £4 per 28 lbs. Many Government ministers had their homes attacked. Lord Palmerston, the war minister ordered his servants to pepper the faces of the mob. And the minister responsible for the Corn bill, Frederick Robinson, and the vice-president of the board of trade had their homes attacked by a mob of rioters. As a result three soldiers and a butler fired into the crowd causing the death of a number of people. However, on the other hand, the farmers who produced Corn in the U.K. believed that imports of Corn would force down prices and as a result it would curtail profits.

In 1817 strict laws were introduced to curb public disorder. This was done because the Government feared revolutionary movements. Even peaceful demonstrations were forced to disperse by the troops. Spinners and weavers combined together and marched on London to petition the Prince Regent. However they were stopped by troops at Stockport and the leaders of the march were arrested.

In 1818 Cotton workers were to go on strike for more money. Although the Combination Acts were in force to prevent groups of workers uniting for a common cause and delegates from towns in the West Country and the North who were Textile workers would go to London to try and form a General Union. They were hoping to form a general union of various trades. However this proved to be unsuccessful and many leaders including those who represented the Spinners were jailed for exciting unrest. Failure was inevitable due to the poor conditions and the shortage of food and as a result the workers began to fear for the well being of their families. Nevertheless, workers in the Textile trades and in other trades were determined to find a way of improving their livelihood and they began to form Friendly Societies. The Foresters were the biggest Society during this period. The Societies would collect a weekly subscription from their members and some Societies would amalgamate in order to attain some stability. We shall see in the next Chapter that it was not only the workers but also the masters would begin to find hardship during the mid 19th century.

Chapter Nine

••••••••••••••••••••••••••

The Decline In The Cloth & Textile Industries

During the early part of the reign of Queen Victoria and during the Premiership of Melbourne (1835 to 1846) and later Peel (1841 to 1846) Timothy Exell became a prominent Orator and writer in support of the Weavers and their plight during the 19th century. Timothy Exell was of the Parish of North Nibley that is situated near Wotton-under-Edge in the district of Dursley in Gloucestershire. He wrote a brief history concerning the Weavers of Gloucestershire to Her Majesty's Commissioner. This full historical report may be seen in the Gloucester Record Office.

In his report he gives reference to the good days between 1563 and 1802. Queen Elizabeth 1 had made certain social reforms in order to help the Poor and unemployed. There were three main laws introduced to prevent monopoly of weavers and manufacturers. A manufacturer would be allowed to operate one loom whilst the weaver could use two looms and use these looms in their cottages. The third rule encouraged those who wanted to take up the trade of weaver should firstly serve an apprenticeship of at least 7 years or serve in Her Majesty's Army as was seen in the Statute of Apprentices of 1563. The Poor Law was also instituted during Her reign in 1601.

During the reign of King George 11 in 1728 the Magistrates at Gloucester fixed the Weaver's wages. And by 15th October 1756 the Weavers and Clothiers formed an alliance and agreed a set wage together with other agreements. It was a period of good fortune in and around Gloucestershire. However by 1802 the Clothiers had combined with members of Parliament to introduce new legislation. As a result the Protection Laws were suspended. When the System of Apprentices was stopped and the manufacturers began to take control of the Weavers livelihood it resulted in much distress and hardship for the Weavers and their families. The Weavers had the option of working in Factories or not working at all. The Manufacturers had the upper hand. They were forced to work long hours for less wages.

Nevertheless there were those Clothiers and manufacturers who tried to help their employees. One such employer was an Edward Sheppard of Uley. By 4th May 1828 Edward Sheppard was Chairman of the Clothiers Committee and he introduced new deals with his workers. These new proposals were greatly acceptable to the Weavers of the Dursley district of Gloucestershire. The new wage structure had been accepted by most Clothiers except for some within the Stroud area and this included Wotton-under-Edge.

For a good many years after 1828 the manufacturers of Cloth wished to reduce more and more their employers wages. It was Timothy Exell who pleaded with the Government to intervene against oppression and to introduce new Legislation that would prove fair to both Masters and Workers. It was necessary to create harmony amongst the Masters and Workers if the Cloth Industry was to survive. Alas this was not to be achieved for sometime. Meanwhile rioters throughout the United Kingdom were attacking factories and machinery. We may remember that after the war with France there was less need for the production of Military uniforms and with military men no longer needed there became, after 1815, a vast number of unemployed. In addition to this the export trade was faltering as was seen in exports to Europe and the U.S.A. Although the U.K. was well known for its fine quality Cloth production, we find that Europe was selling more at a reduced price. Because of the state of the economy in other parts of the world it became inevitable that other Countries like the U.S. sought cheaper goods.

The Cottage Industry

The Carding and the Spinning of Wool was done, as in the Hating Industry from home during the 18th century to the beginning of the 19th century. It was later that Manufacturers began employing more into their Factories and the Cottage Industries were to become obsolete. The Weavers and Spinners operated from their cottages. After their apprenticeship they would qualify as Journeymen if they did not become themselves Masters of their trade. These Journeymen were self-employed and sometimes you would see them operating as a family unit. These tradesmen would do work for various Clothiers and seek work by travelling to and from factories in order to procure work.

When Journeymen became Clothiers and Masters of their trade they would also be seen travelling to procure work and they would send agents to various parts of the Country. They would purchase wool from the sheep farmers and employ persons to weave and prepare the wool for sale to the Blackwell Hall Factors who were London based and agents for the export trade. Those who possessed larger premises usually did the dying and finishing, while the fulling part of the process was done in the Factories. However when machines were introduced it became necessary for the whole process to be done in the factory units.

A Carding Engineer Dresser was responsible for the maintenance of the factory machinery and he would usually be called out to various factories as self-employed. He would move about from place to place as a Journeyman. He would prepare the alignment for the process to begin. One such Carding Engineer Dresser was Jacob Salter who was born at Frampton Cotterell and later moved with his parents, George and Margaret Salter, to Kingswood in Wiltshire that is now in the County of Gloucestershire. He worked within the districts of Stroud and Dursley in Gloucestershire.

The Salter, Webb, Cole, Bartlett, Sheppard, Hale, Whitaker and Rossiter families are recorded as far back as the seventeenth century as being connected in some way to the Cloth Industries in Cornwall, Dorset, Devon, Somerset, Wiltshire and Gloucestershire. In the beginning it was not unusual for Clothiers to be associated with land-ownership. Clothiers would very often purchase in a number of towns and villages factories for fulling. These factories were to be known as Fulling Mills. The owner of the Fulling Mills would lease out their buildings to others and this is seen also in the fact that relatives would be given the opportunity to lease these Mills. An example of this may be seen in a Westbury Clothier by the name of Whitaker who built a new mill at Eddington in 1519. He later would lease this Mill to others.

Transport was not as it is to-day, but it appears that families were quite extensively large and they would incorporate into their business not only their own kin but would bring together their cousins and in-laws from afar. This shows that although travel from one place to another took longer kinship was close. One example is seen in the Cole family from America when they sent their daughter, Mary A. Cole in the summer of 1877 to Bristol at the age of 17 years to visit her uncle and cousins the Salter's. During her stay in the U.K. she was taken to Devon and Cornwall by horse drawn carriage in order to visit her relations there. She kept a diary of the sea crossing and her stay in the U.K. A copy of this diary may be seen in Bristol Record Office and Chapter twelve of this Book together with a detailed account of their cousins from Gloucestershire.

The means of commercial transport of Textiles and other commodities through the U.K. was by means of horsedrawn carriages or in some cases the transport of salt on mules until the Canals were constructed in the mid eighteenth century. However these canals or inland waterways were intended to carry heavier goods such as tin, timber and coal to various parts of the U.K. A famous engineer constructed the first waterway in 1759 by the name of Brindley. This waterway was built between Manchester and Bridgewater. In order to allow the barges to rise and fall over the land locks were introduced for this purpose. The barges would enter a lock. Large thick gates would close in order to seal the lock. The lock would then be filled with water raising the barge to the next level up stream. The reverse would be required to allow the barge to descend the various levels of land en route. In 1767 the Manchester and Liverpool canal link was started and the Forth/Clyde Canal was started in 1768. It was not long after this that there were a number of canal links in the U.K., Ireland and Scotland.

Canals were still being built in Queen Victoria's reign and they were being used not only for merchandize but also for military and shipping purposes.

As we have noted in earlier chapters there have been a number of innovations during the 18th century. In the Textile Trades we see revolutionary methods of production by way of machinery. In 1733 Kay invented the flying-shuttle that was to revolutionize the method of weaving. Hargreaves invented the spinning Jenny in 1764 and in 1769 we see the new method of spinning through rollers that were powered by water. By 1782 a man named Watt invented the Steam engine. Steam engines became a new means for operating machinery including shipping and in 1814 we see the invention of the first locomotive by Stephenson. By 1825 the first railway was opened between Stockton and Darlington.

Although the introduction of the Railways and the construction of better road ways – the canals although still partly in use were being bought up by the railway Companies and many were closed to reduce competition with the railways – we need to briefly examine the economical state of the Country in order to ascertain the reasons for the decline in the manufacture of Textiles.

The introduction of machinery into factories was to prove an asset in producing goods at a greater pace incurring more profits and enabling the economy to benefit both management and worker. Nevertheless in the beginning it seemed to workers that machinery was the cause of much hardship.

During the war year's industries found prosperity and as a result wages rose sharply. However the cost of living was getting more expensive and this caused in many cases starvation for the poorer classes. Riots became inevitable due to the poor having little help from the Government of the day and the fear of the new machinery. Ned Ludd was a villager of little means and of little education but it was not long before he formed many followers that became known as the "Luddite Movement". They became violent demonstrators and were responsible for much damage to machinery and factory buildings. The handloom workers were finding living conditions very hard because they had to compete with the power-loom that had recently been introduced. The weavers were also finding it hard to make a living. In 1797 a skilled weaver was earning 26 shillings and 8 pence a week but by 1811 their wages had dropped considerable to only 14 shillings and 7 pence a week. However the poor did have some support in Parliament in the person of Lord Byron who pleaded their stricken cause in the House of Lords. He showed much mercy and in some way understanding with regard to the rioters and those demanding better living conditions. But not so with the Judges who were want to give severe sentences to rioters and the like. One example is the sentence handed out to a young boy of fifteen who was a sentry or lookout for some rioters. He was sentenced to death for his part in this particular riot and on the scaffold he pleaded to his mother for help who in turn was unable to help her son.

As the situation for the poor of society worsened more people became agitated at their plight, especially as it seemed that the Government were in fact making things worse for the poor in the land by new legislation and restricted the middle class and the poor from having a say in matters that were essential to their well being and livelihood. Although Lord Wellington, who became Prime Minister in 1828 had been a hero in the war with Napoleon of France he was not a good statesman and by 1830 he was replaced by Lord Grey. It is said that the reason for Wellington's fall from office was due to his lack of consideration for the poor and his refusal to accept reform that became necessary if the Cloth Industry was to survive and the economical state of the Country was to change for the benefit of all classes.

Nevertheless it was during the Premiership of Liverpool between 1812 and 1827 and the reign of George 111 and George IV that the repressive policies of the Government were introduced. The Habeas Corpus was suspended in 1817 that had been introduced previously to protect the poor. There were also six Acts of Parliament that became known as the Gagging Acts. These six were as follows.

1. An Act to suppress unauthorized military drilling.
2. An Act prescribing harsh penalties for libel such as any malicious publications against the state or insurrection that could result in a revolution as was seen in France.
3. An Act suppressing freedom of the Press.
4. An Act to suppress seditious meetings and thus curb freedom of speech.
5. An Act to authorize magistrates to check personal liberty and to prevent any uprising by the seizure of arms.
6. An Act to take immediate steps in crimes of violence and bring the culprits to justice.

It was during this period after the war years that the Cloth Industries saw the decline in manufacture and unemployment. Only a few Clothiers and Manufacturers of Textile products were fortunate to survive these difficult times. The labourers were hard hit by the abolition of income tax and it was replaced by high taxes on the necessities of life such as soap, candles, paper, sugar, beer and tobacco as well as the basic essentials on the food front – bread and potatoes. In addition the Poor Law Relief rates were cut causing much hardship amongst the poor families. There were also calls for the reform of the Elizabethan Poor Law for parish relief of poverty. Although Chartism was partly formed as a political movement its aims were also to show the plight of the poor and their appalling conditions.

Vincent, the editor of the Western Vindicator and the Gloucestershire Magistrates would agree on different standpoints, emphasising the low pay of the workforce as the main course of the disputes at this time. Vincent was to monitor any successful meetings in the Cloth Manufacturing areas and he would sometimes use inflammatory language against the oppressors of the workers in order to prove a point. However, the Whigs, an old English Party that upheld popular rights and in some way was the forerunners of reform. By 1832 the Tories, who were landowners and who were originally against reform, now took up the cause for the poor in the persons of William 1V, and Lord Grey who brought to Parliament his famous Reform Bill, whose aim was to enfranchise the middle classes. On this first attempt it was accepted in the House of Commons only to be rejected in the House of Lords. The voice of the people having been denied rouse up by marching to London and rioting throughout the Country broke out. Bristol also showed their objections to the rejection of the Reform Bill and Birmingham threatened to send 20 thousand marchers to London to protest. Nevertheless by 1832 the amended Bill was passed. It may be of worthy note that the introduction of new Liberal Peers to the House of Lords would produce a majority vote in favour of the Bill. This was not the complete answer to the difficulties in the domestic affairs of the United Kingdom but only the beginnings.

Hard times were to force parents to send their children of a young age to work in the Factories and some would be sent at the early age of 6 years in order to produce more money into the household and thereby have sufficient funds to buy bread and potatoes that were part of the main diet of the poorer families. In order to tackle this problem the new Whig (Liberal) reforming Government under Grey and Melbourne introduced a new Act of Parliament that became known as the Factory Act of 1833. This Act however dealt only with the Textile Trades such as cotton and woollen fabrics. It was forbidden to allow children under the age of 9 to work in Factories and that any child under the age of 13 years would only be allowed to work not more than 48 hours in week and only up to 9 hours per day. This resulted in higher wages for the adult workforce and helped to increase the purchasing power of the workers. Four Inspectors were created to inspect the Factories and to ensure that the owners of the Textile Factories adhered to the new legislation.

In the same year that the new Factory Act of 1833 (replacing the 1819) became law, Uley, Dursley and Wotton-under-Edge received their first visit by the Factories Commissioners in 1833. They were to report that there were a large number of Mills that had ceased production. They had found that out of the nineteen names they had been given only twelve manufacturers remained to produce their Textile products. Some had retired prematurely due to failure in trade whilst others had become bankrupt. Out of the bankruptcies only two were officially recorded and the others had come to some agreement with their Creditors.

There are a number of reasons why so many Manufacturers were losing business in the Textile Trade. One was due to the export trade. The Americans had imposed heavy duties on wool imported from the United Kingdom. This created a heavy burden on the U.K. export trade. Another factor was the aftermath of the War years where unemployment rose sharply and there became less need for mass production of the uniform. Due to the adverse circumstances that prevailed in the Textile Industries many manufacturers decided to retire early rather than face bankruptcy. They put their money into various investments and they were then able to live reasonably well. There is one example of a manufacturer, R.S. Culicott of Weston Mills that is situated near Bath in Somerset, who endeavoured to sell his Mill but failed and as a result he became bankrupt in 1825. However the cloth known as Cassimere proved popular and became an asset to the Textile Trade. The many bankruptcies, especially around Gloucestershire were to help the remaining Cloth Manufacturers to increase their trade and therefore make a reasonable to excellent profit margin. However, whilst the towns of Radwick and Coaley were to see much unemployment there was still more Cloth produced in this region. By 1893 a Bradford Manufacturer once said that he had experienced good trade and more employed within the Textile Trade. Steam power proved an asset to trade in the Yorkshire dales and as a result manufacturers were able to produce their goods at a cheaper rate than in other parts of the United Kingdom.

Some manufacturers were finding it hard to pay their wage bills. Child cheap labour had decreased as a result of the new Statutes of Parliament and this resulted in the increase of Adult wages. William Playne of Longford Mill closed his factory rather than pay the extra wage bills. This proved inevitable in many other cases. However overseas trade appeared to remain stable especially in the Cloth exports to China. Nevertheless trade in some cases was in the exchange of goods rather than that of cash. An example of this may be seen in the firm of T. & S.S. Marling of Ebley Mill who were manufacturing cloth for export. In 1841 they had sent cloths to Canton in China and they had expected in return other goods to the value of £9,000. Reports of the trade with China may be seen in the Gloucestershire Journal dated 8th and 29th January 1848. Thomas Marling showed confidence in the textile trades in Stroud district when he made his report to the Parliamentary Committee on the Bristol to Birmingham Railway Bill. During this debate it was claimed that Trade in the Trowbridge and Bradford areas of Wiltshire were doing better than Gloucestershire. Traders in the County of Wiltshire were doing better in their trade with Ireland. In fact, J. Blake and Benjamin Copper of Staverton Mill told another Committee that the bulk of his firm's output went to Bristol for Liverpool and then to Ireland. However when Charles Stevens of Stanley Mills was questioned concerning the Cheltenham and the Great Western Union Railway in 1836, he said that Gloucestershire was holding supremacy over that of Yorkshire Cloth. He, like Marling believed that trade was good and producing more in and around Gloucestershire.

Some Woollen Traders began to believe that there was still hope in the Industry and where others had failed due to bankruptcy, these traders persevered and suceeded. In the Gloucester Journal dated 3rd August 1837 there appeared an advert with the initial W.S.P., asking for a partner who had the sum of £4,000 to £5,000 to invest into a small but a very respectable Woollen Factory. Nevertheless, those who did venture to invest into what appeared to be a good enterprise were to fail by the mid 1830's and the firm that they had invested in became bankrupt. An example may be seen in the Mill owned by Hicks of Eastington who became bankrupt in 1835. And by 1837 a well-known trader by the name of Edward Sheppard of Uley in Gloucestershire was to become bankrupt. It may be noted that the Sheppard and Salter families originated from Devon, as did the Slade Family and became close friends and some were linked through marriage. Edward Sheppard had tried to keep his 'head above water' in the endeavour to reduce his wages bill but as a result it created more difficulties when the workers threatened strike action. He eventually came to a compromise with his workers, but this did not change the inevitable outcome.

It has been said that over trading in 1832 was partly to blame for the failures and difficulties during 1839 and beyond. It was evident that those people that took much capital out of their business to support high living consumption were those who actually failed. However those who took little out of their business and re-invested proved more successful. Another factor was seen in the Credit agreements between the Clothiers and their Agents, the Blackwell Hall Factors of London. This firm expected large sums in commission/interest on loans and extended credit. It was not long before the Clothiers and Cloth Manufacturers began to deal direct with their customers. The long credit arrangements and the large sums for commission by the Blackwell Hall Factors was blamed for the many bankruptcies in the Textile Industries. During the depression from the late autumn of 1836 to 1842 some Banks were also finding difficulties in that they too suffered loses in revenue and as a result they had to close. One such Bank was Hobhouse & Company of Bath. They had helped to support two large factories, the Coopers of Staverton and Saunders of Bradford. Thus, during the depression trade was not good and therefore the flow of money was depreciating for the Banks.

Some of the Salter's of Wiltshire survived the depression whilst others had to sell. The Webb families of Gloucestershire and especially that of the Stroud Valley were also successful. The Salter's of Wiltshire and Gloucestershire became united in marriage and in some cases an added dowry to the family assets improved their status.

Although we see the Textile Industry showing good returns the decline had already started in the mid 18th century. The East India Company were in financial trouble as early as July 1772 and was on the verge of bankruptcy. So bad was the financial situation that the Directors asked the government to defer the payment of £203,000 now due to the customs for excise duties. On top of the collapse of commercial confidence, which followed the slump in Europe, the Company had grave problems of its own. The cost of living had increased dramatically due to the war in India with the Princes and the famine in Bengal. The directors of the Company had put the dividend to 12.5% that they thought unwisely that this would help to rectify the grave situation. In the face of mismanagement and financial irregularities in the Company's activities the U.K. Government made a new Regulating Act in order to control their dealings by forcing them to reduce their high dividends. In response the East India Company reduced the high dividend and they accepted new Supreme Council in Bengal whose members were to be nominated by the British Government. The Company agreed to all of this, as they needed a loan from the Government in order to keep afloat of the current situation. However, by August 1858 the Company was abolished, and the Government under the Premiership of Derby-Disraili and the reign of Queen Victoria took full control of the Company and their assets.

There were other firms that went bankrupt in the 18th century. To name but a few there was Anstie, junior acquired a Dye house within the Snakemead Mill in Devizes, Wiltshire from Bridget, the daughter of William Green of Salisbury. However by 1793 Anstie had become bankrupt and within two years the new owners, Julius Samuel Rich and Thomas Timbrell of Trowbridge were experiencing problems. Rich was in partnership with Heapy and the firm was known as Rich and Heapy, Blackwell Hall factors. They went bankrupt in 1795 and it became necessary for Timbrell to buy Rich's share and in 1797 sold to James White and Jonas Fish of Devizes who were clothiers but by the following year in 1798 they too went bankrupt. Clothiers would often keep separate their Dye Houses from their Factories. This may be seen in the Salter's of Trowbridge and the Sheppard's at Frome. Dye Houses needed clean water and therefore it was better management to keep these businesses away from the factory in order to specialize. Many Clothiers found it beneficial to work these Dye Houses on a commission basis. Clothiers would also endeavour to rent rather than own the property, as they would have less expenditure in the long run. Another dyer by the name of John Bartlett of Chippenham had taken on a lease in 1822 from Uriah Tarrant. However within 3 years he had also become bankrupt and unable to pay his debts he was sent to prison in 1825. John Bartlett was the last dyer to operate on this site and the premises were later to become private dwellings that were named Parry's Yard. By the 19th century the Textile trade was very much in decline and perhaps one of the reasons that the Dye House business did not survive many years before becoming bankrupt was the fact that there were too many of them being established especially within the Counties of Gloucestershire, Wiltshire and Somerset.

It was not unusual for Premises to be occupied by more than one Lessee and for it to be used for several purposes. One example is of Waterford Mill at Chippenham. A photo of this Mill may be seen in the Chippenham Museum. The Mill and Factory premises was, according to the rate returns of 1811 and 1812 owned by Thomas Bailey who ran a tannery business attached to the Mill, and the Mill Factory was occupied by George Austin and Company who were trading in Cloth. Austin was also associated with Wotton-under-Edge in Gloucestershire and his daughter was to marry into the Salter family. They were trading in the Textile Industry within the County of Gloucestershire. In 1815 the new Clothing Factory that had been recently erected was sold together with steam engine, water wheel, mill tackle, a counting house, a dye-house and drying stove. It was sold to John Saunders and Thomas Hosier Saunders of Bradford and Charles Salter Taylor of Chippenham who were established Clothiers. It was purchased for £460 with an annuity of £250 to Thomas Bailey and his wife for the remainder of their lives. By 1816 the new partnership purchased a smaller Woollen Factory in Back Lane from Christopher and Ann Heath. John Heath had built it in 1814. The partnership ran the business under the name of C. S. Taylor and Company. By 1816 they had 100 persons employed by them. They had ventured into another enterprise at Malmesbury. However this was to prove too big an adventure and as a result Taylor became bankrupt in 1830 and he was forced to sell the extensive property with all its equipment.

Looking on the brighter side of events in the Textile Industries we can see examples of those Companies that were successful. Ephraim Salter was born in the Parish of Bathford in Somerset, the son of a hosier of that County. In the last quarter of the 18th century he moved to Trowbridge to seek his fortune in the Clothing trade and he became a successful businessman. On the 23rd June 1772 he married Margaret Webb of Trowbridge at Saint James Parish Church in Trowbridge, Wiltshire. It had been stated by Canon Jackson that he was poor and that he did not even have sixpence to his name. However, his family from Bath were middle class and they were not short of a bob or two, in fact it was not long before Ephraim was to become a partner with William Dunn as Clothiers in Trowbridge. This partnership lasted until 1794 when Ephraim Salter traded independently. His son, Samuel Salter, became a partner in the firm. However, after the liquidation of the partnership of Ephraim Salter and William Dunn both parties remained associated with the premises in Fore Street. Their had been three Clothiers houses in Fore Street and they were numbers 1 to 3 and these were owned by the Mortimer family and leased out to the Salter and Dunn family. In 1807 William Dunn purchased numbers 2 and 3 and used the workshops behind these premises. He also owned property in Court Street. Ephraim and Samuel Salter occupied number 8 Fore Street. Ephraim died there in 1821 and his son Samuel became sole proprietor of the Clothing business and before his death in 1850 acquired more and more buildings that covered the site in Fore Street. Samuel also had connections in Wotton-under-Edge in Gloucestershire.

As we look more closely, we find that the families associated with the Cloth Industries within Wiltshire and Gloucestershire originated from Somerset and further West towards Dorset, Devon and Cornwall. Ephraim Salter was born in Bath in Somerset and as we know became a successful Clothier in Wiltshire. Another family from Somerset have their roots in Frome, Somerset and that is the Sheppard families who also became successful in the Clothing trade. A descendent of the Frome family is Edward Sheppard of Uley in Gloucestershire who also became successful as a Clothier. Hutchens Mill was part of the Longleat estate in 1681 and was converted for cloth working and enlarged in 1793 and Sheppard's of Frome subsequently leased it. However in 1810 there was a serious fire in the Mill that caused the rebuilding of the site. After it was rebuilt by 1812 a farmer by the name of William Webb of Roddenbury leased it but soon after William Webb was found murdered and as a result the Factory was sold in 1814 and the Sheppards who had previously leased the site now became the owners. The Sheppards had run a successful business at Rodden until 1860 and in 1873 it was sold to William Beauchamp of Frome, a coal merchant. He is recorded in the Directory of 1875 as being the proprietor of the Frome Woollen Mills. This Mill however closed in 1883.

Another family that moved from Frome, Somerset was that of the Rossiter family who migrated to South Wales in the turn of the 20th century. One of the descendents is Sheila Davies of Saint Mellons near Cardiff. She was born in Newport, Monmouthshire, now in the County of Gwent. Her grandfather was a William Rossiter of Frome whose father was also named William. This William was born about 1820 at Frome. He married and had two sons, William and Frederick who were both Quarrymen. William was born about 1848 and Frederick was born about 1850 and married Annie Lane in Frome. Both William and Frederick moved to Newport in 1901. William married and had two sons, Clarence and Ivor Rossiter. Ivor married and he had two daughters, Sheila and Marjorie (known as Marge). Sheila married Alfred George Davies at Saint Mary's Catholic Church, Stow Hill in Newport. They had two sons, Michael and Jeffrey, and one daughter Helen.

A William Rossiter of Adderwell in Frome owned property; a Mill and known as "Bellis Hole". Samuel Seviour occupied this Mill. William Rossiter was a Clothier and he had traded under the name of William and John Rossiter (John being his brother) operated their business from Keyford and it is more than probable that they had use of the Adderwell Mills. These Mills were in operation until 1848 when they stopped production. By 1853 the Upper Mill had been converted into a block of houses but although the lower Mill was not working William and John Rossiter still owned this property. The Upper Mill can be seen now as a Georgian house of two storeys with attics, whilst the Lower Mill became a Dyewood and Chemical Works and became known as "Providence Mills".

With the decline of the Cloth Industries within Gloucestershire, Somerset and Wiltshire, the Salter families began to look elsewhere in the Textile trade in order to make a profit. It was probably best to have ones eggs in more than one basket. In other words stay within the trade but expand so that one would not only produce fine cloths but also make the material into fine and acceptable clothing. As we will see in the next Chapter most of the Salter's from Kingswood and the Stroud district of South Gloucestershire were to expand into the Tailoring trade.

John Salter was a successful Clothier. He had been apprenticed in the early part of the 19th century as a Woollen Spinner but he decided to apprentice his children to be tailors. William, his younger son was apprenticed to his uncle in Coleford. John's younger brother, Charles had apprenticed his son George in the same trade. Likewise, John's father Jacob Salter was a Carding Engineer Dresser but realising the difficulties the Cloth Trade was facing encouraged his children to follow in the tailoring trade. His descendents were to become successful tailors up until the 1950's, as we shall see in the next Chapter.

Chapter 10

The Salter's become Tailors and migrate across the Severn Estuary to the Forest of Dean in Gloucestershire

The Salter and the Bartlett families of Devon were landowners, and some were trading as Millers/bakers, Shop Keepers, Mariners, whilst others were Ministers of Religion. The Miller/baker branches of the family were from South Devon, Exeter, Sandford and Ottery-St. Mary regions. The Salter families and also the Cole, Slade, Bartlett families were to move from Devon into Somerset, Wiltshire, Gloucestershire, London and Liverpool.

George Salter was the descendent of Rev. John Salter of South Devon in Saint Marychurch near Torquay. He moved to Wiltshire where he married Margaret Axton on the 21st March 1774. They had ten children and lived for 15 years in Frampton-Cotterell until 1790 when they moved to Kingswood, Wiltshire (that is now in Gloucestershire since 1844) that is situated near to Wotton-under-Edge in Gloucestershire. Whilst living in Frampton-Cotterell he leased Mill premises from Thomas Blanchard in 1780 and the spelling of his surname was recorded in the Land Tax Records as 'Saulter'. Their sons were apprenticed to the Bakery business and the Textile trades. The following is a short introduction to their children.

1. James, the first son of George and Margaret Salter was born on 10th July 1774. Little is known of James Salter.
2. Their second son, Isaac was baptized on 17th March 1776 at Frampton-Cotterell, South Gloucestershire. He died in 1857 and he is buried with his brother Charles in the Family Grave at the Rowland Hill Tabernacle Church Yard in Wotton-under-Edge. He became a Master Hatter by trade and he married and had issue.
3. Their third son George was baptized on the 16th August 1778 at Frampton-Cotterell. There is no further reference to this George so it is assumed that he died young.
4. Their fourth son George, who became known as Charles was baptized on 5th March 1780 at Frampton-Cotterell. Charles became a Baker by trade and later in about 1826 he became an Itinerant Lay Preacher for the Congregational (Presbyterian) Chapel in Wotton-under-Edge. He died on 28th November 1856 at the age of 76 and he is buried in the Family Grave. Full details of his

family may be seen in the second Book entitled 'The Salter Archives from 1211'.

5.   Jacob, the son of George and Margaret Salter, was born on 22ⁿᵈ February 1782. He married Mary Trull, the daughter of John & Anne (nee Tipping Trull) on the 26ᵗʰ December 1803. Witnesses to the wedding were Martha Trull the sister of Mary Trull and William Perrin the brother-in-Law of Jacob Salter and the husband of Esther Trull. William Perrin was a Wool Manufacturer and his Mill is situated a few miles outside of Dursley on the Uley Road. The Mill is now a Farm and it is called 'Mill Farm'. Jacob became a Carding Engineer Dresser by trade but later joined his brother Charles in the shop at 4 Bear Street in Wotton-under-Edge. Jacob had some foresight in the knowledge that while the Cloth Industry was in decline there would always be the need for professional Tailors so he apprenticed some of his children to become associated with the Tailoring trade. Full details of his marriage and his in-laws may be seen in the second Book, 'The Salter Archives from 1211'.

Jacob Salter in 1860

Bear Street
in Wotton-Under-Edge,
Gloucestershire

6. Sarah, the daughter of George and Margaret Salter, was born in 1782 and she was baptized on 20th July 1783 at Frampton-Cotterell. She died young and she was buried in 1785.

7. Sally/Sarah Salter was born in 1784 and she was baptized on 22nd May 1785 at Frampton-Cotterell. She became known as Sarah after the sudden death of her sister. She married John, the son of Samuel Webb a Clothier near Stroud, on the 30th March 1807 at Wotton-under-Edge and they had issue. They had a son whom they baptized as Jacob Henry Webb on 15th August 1822 at Avening Forest Green Chapel. He became a Schoolmaster in the Parish of Saint Michael Coventry and where he met his future wife. He married Elizabeth Seager, the daughter of William Seager at the Parish Church of Saint Martin in Birmingham, Warwickshire on 20th January 1847. They later moved to the Bahamas with their two children and he became an Inspector of Schools and he was later promoted to a Government Office as a Civil Servant. Full details together with a copy letter of Jacob Henry Webb may be seen in the second Book, 'Salter Archives from 1211'.

8. David, the son of George and Margaret (nee Axton) Salter, was born about 1786/7 and he was baptized on 24th June 1787 at Frampton-Cotterell. He became a Cloth-Finisher by trade. He married Anne Tidman on the 28th October 1813 at Wotton-under-Edge in Gloucestershire where they had issue.

9. Mary was born about 1789 and she was baptized on 10th February 1790. She died 19th December 1860 at the age of 70 years.

It was in the next generation that we actually find the children of the above becoming associated with the Tailoring Industry. Charles's son George was born in June 1813 and he was baptized in August 1813 at the Congregational Chapel in Wotton-under-Edge. He was probably one of the first of the family to become a Tailor and he operated his business within Wotton-under-Edge. He married Elizabeth Peglar at Kingswood on the 15th July 1832. However there is some discrepancy with the census records that names his wife as Emma.

Jacob and Mary (nee Trull) Salter's children were either apprenticed to their grandfathers' trade as Bakers and Grocers, whilst the other children followed their father in the Textile Trade as Clothiers, and in the next generation as Tailors. Their children are seen in the following trades.

1. James, the son of Jacob & Mary (nee Trull) Salter, was born 3rd November 1804 at Abbey Cottages, Kingswood, Wiltshire. He married Elizabeth and lived in Long Street, Wotton-under-Edge where they had a Tea and Grocery shop. It is now a Tea and Cake shop selling afternoon teas. James died on the 16th November 1895 at the age of 91 in High Street, Stonehouse in Gloucestershire.

2.   John was born 23rd June 1806 at Abbey Cottages, Kingswood, Wiltshire. After his apprenticeship he became a Woollen Spinner and Clothier within the Wotton and North Nibley areas. He married Elizabeth Pick of Cromhall on 2nd May 1831 at The Church of Saint Mary The Virgin in Kingswood. The Rev. Thomas Thomas officiated. John later joined the Baptist Church and he was re-baptized in the Independent Chapel where his uncle Charles was a Lay Preacher. Their youngest son, William Salter, became a Master Tailor. William was born in 1847 in Gloucester Road, North Nibley. At the age of fourteen years he was apprenticed to his Uncle Charles and the younger brother of John at the Tailors shop in Saint John Street, Coleford, the Forest of Dean, Gloucestershire. He did his final year apprenticeship with his cousin Hubert Salter at 11 Saint James Churchyard in Bristol. He married Eliza Furney, the daughter of Robert Furney, a Hatter by trade in Reading, Berkshire. The family lived for a couple of years at Aylesbury in Buckinghamshire before moving to Coleford where they took up residence at 30 Boxbush Road and later started a Drapery and Tailor business at 1 Boxbush Road, Coleford. Their first child, Maude Louisa was born in Aylesbury on 12th August 1872. See Salter's Archives for more details.

Photo taken in Cheltenham in 1886 of Richard Tipping Salter.
Born 5/7/1814 died 25/11/1891.

3.   Richard Tipping Salter, the son of Jacob and Mary (nee Trull) Salter, was born 5th July 1814 at Abbey Cottages, Kingswood and he died on the 25th November 1891 at the age of 77. He was buried in the Cheltenham Cemetery, Gloucestershire. He was the first of this family to move across the Severn Estuary and into the Forest of Dean. He was apprenticed to a Tailor in Kingswood, Wiltshire and he moved to Coleford in 1837 when he became a Master Tailor. He married Harriett, the daughter of George (a carpenter by trade) and Eleanor Jones, on the 29th May 1837 at Abenhall Parish Church that is situated near Cinderford in the Forest of Dean in Gloucestershire. Their sons Rowland Hill (Richard), and Hubert were apprenticed to their father as Tailors. They had six children and their youngest son Joseph who was born in 1849 became a Painter by trade. The family lived at the Poolway on the Gloucester Road. Here they brought up their family in the Baptist tradition and practised their faith at the Baptist Chapel, Newland Road, Coleford. Newland Road is situated just off Market and Saint John Street. Richard was noted for his piety and this was reflected in the families' togetherness throughout the day. He taught the family to pray together before and after meals. Later generations were to follow his example. He was seen to retire after lunch and dinner for a quiet recollection and meditation for at least 20 to 30 minutes each day. Whenever time would permit between his trading as a Draper and Tailor he would preach at various Chapels around the Forest including Symonds Yat, Parkend, Redbrook, Penalt and several other places.

Below is a photo of the Baptist Church at Symonds Yat.

Details of Richard Tipping and Harriet (nee Jones) children can be read in the Salter Archives from 1211. When Harriet died in 1858 at the young age of 44 years. Richard had lost a good wife and mother. However his faith helped him through the empty years ahead. During this period of loss he was comforted by members of the Baptist congregation and during this period he found a special solace in that of Ann Morris the organist of the Baptist Church and on the 2nd March 1861 he married Ann, the aunt of Ben Morris of Coleford. Ann was a Seamstress and the Sunday School Teacher. Richard was 70 when Ann died and in 1884 he retired to Cheltenham to live with his daughter, Selina at 8 Bath Parade. He became a member of the Salem Baptist Church where he is recorded as a member. Also recorded in the Church records is his nephew, William Trull Salter, the son of Charles and Sophia (nee Howell) Salter, who became a member in 1886.

A Picture of William Trull Salter at the age of 19 years

William Trull Salter, the son of Charles and Sophia (nee Howell) Salter, was born 9th April 1867 and the twin of Hubert James Salter. He was apprenticed to the local Printer in Coleford. When he had qualified he left Coleford when he was 19 years and lived with his uncle Richard Tipping Salter and his cousin, Selina in Cheltenham, Gloucestershire. In 1889 and when he was 21 years he left Cheltenham for Cardiff in South Wales to begin a career as a Master Printer. On the 9th September 1893 he married his cousin Julia Jones at Battersea Park Tabernacle in Wandsworth in London. The Jones family were originally of Coleford in Gloucestershire.

The details of William Trull Salter and his descendents may be read in the Salter Archives from 1211.

The chart below shows the family connections with that of Salter, Morgan-Jones and Teague

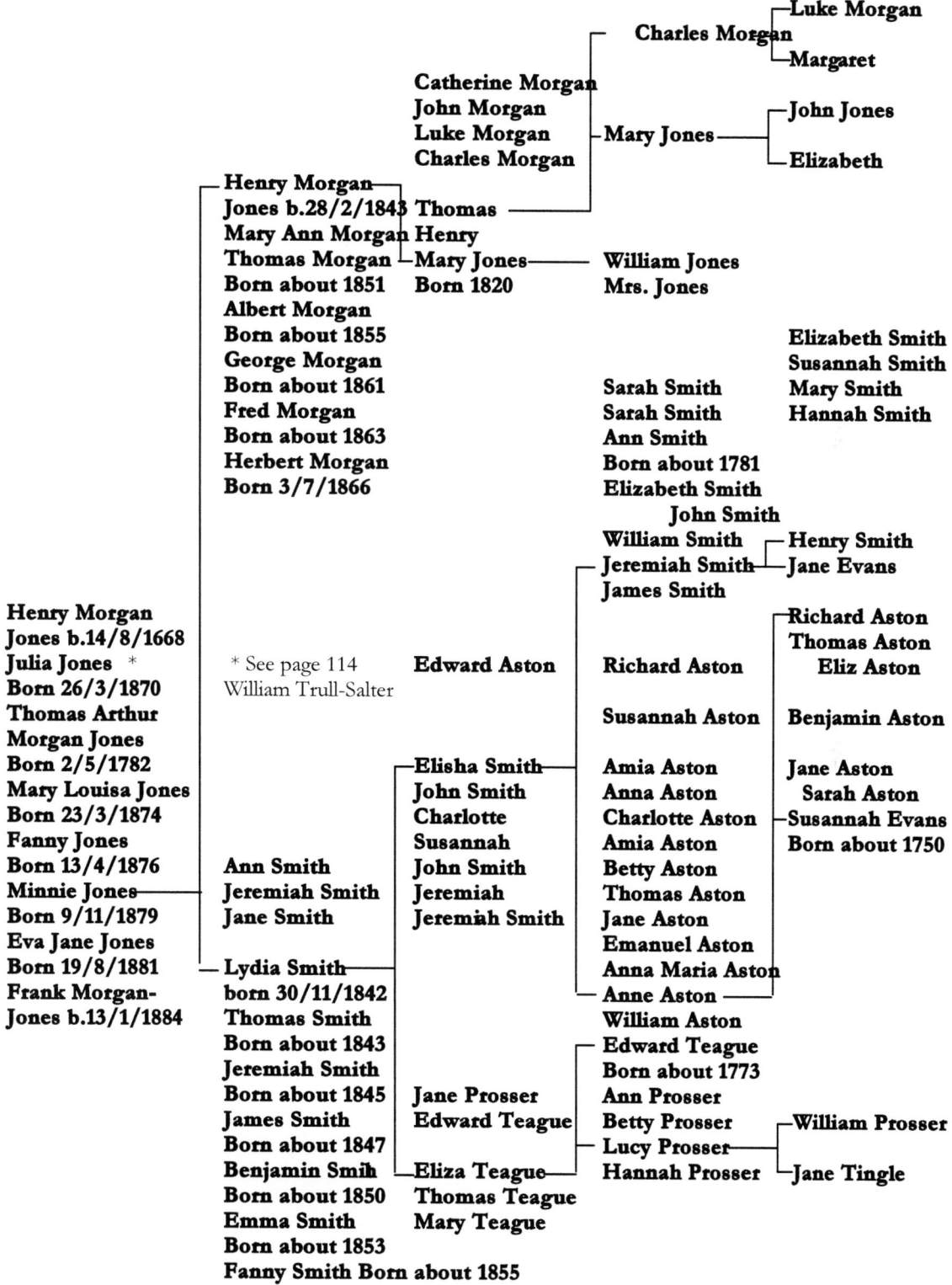

Luke Morgan

Charles Morgan

Margaret

Catherine Morgan
John Morgan
Luke Morgan
Charles Morgan

Mary Jones

John Jones

Elizabeth

Henry Morgan
Jones b.28/2/1843
Mary Ann Morgan
Thomas Morgan
Born about 1851
Albert Morgan
Born about 1855
George Morgan
Born about 1861
Fred Morgan
Born about 1863
Herbert Morgan
Born 3/7/1866

Thomas
Henry
Mary Jones
Born 1820

William Jones
Mrs. Jones

Elizabeth Smith
Susannah Smith
Mary Smith
Hannah Smith

Sarah Smith
Sarah Smith
Ann Smith
Born about 1781
Elizabeth Smith
John Smith
William Smith
Jeremiah Smith
James Smith

Henry Smith
Jane Evans

Henry Morgan
Jones b.14/8/1668
Julia Jones *
Born 26/3/1870
Thomas Arthur
Morgan Jones
Born 2/5/1782
Mary Louisa Jones
Born 23/3/1874
Fanny Jones
Born 13/4/1876
Minnie Jones
Born 9/11/1879
Eva Jane Jones
Born 19/8/1881
Frank Morgan-
Jones b.13/1/1884

* See page 114
William Trull-Salter

Edward Aston

Richard Aston

Susannah Aston

Richard Aston
Thomas Aston
Eliz Aston

Benjamin Aston

Elisha Smith
John Smith
Charlotte
Susannah
John Smith
Jeremiah
Jeremiah Smith

Amia Aston
Anna Aston
Charlotte Aston
Amia Aston
Betty Aston
Thomas Aston
Jane Aston
Emanuel Aston
Anna Maria Aston
Anne Aston
William Aston

Jane Aston
Sarah Aston
Susannah Evans
Born about 1750

Ann Smith
Jeremiah Smith
Jane Smith

Lydia Smith
born 30/11/1842
Thomas Smith
Born about 1843
Jeremiah Smith
Born about 1845
James Smith
Born about 1847
Benjamin Smih
Born about 1850
Emma Smith
Born about 1853
Fanny Smith Born about 1855

Jane Prosser
Edward Teague

Eliza Teague
Thomas Teague
Mary Teague

Edward Teague
Born about 1773
Ann Prosser
Betty Prosser
Lucy Prosser
Hannah Prosser

William Prosser

Jane Tingle

4.   Charles Salter, the youngest son of Jacob and Mary (nee Trull) Salter and the younger brother of Richard Tipping Salter, was born on 24th June 1824 in Abbey Cottages, Kingswood near Wotton-under-Edge in Gloucestershire. After his apprenticeship as a Tailor he went and lived in Long Cross Street in Wotton-under-Edge and he is recorded as living there in the 1851 census. He also became a Master Tailor and he eventually followed his brother and moved to Coleford. He first traded and lived at 10 Saint John Street in Coleford and he later acquired premises at 17 Saint John Street and 121 Market Place. And the family also had premises at 46 Newland Road. On the 14th February 1852 he married Sophia (sometimes known as Sarah), the daughter of George Howell the local postman, at Newland Road Baptist Chapel. Charles later became a deacon in the Baptist Church. Details of the family may be seen in the Salter Archives from 1211. Reference is also made in Cyril Harts book on the History of Coleford pages 217/8. Charles wrote an obituary in the Coleford Baptist Visitor of 1900 for his deceased brother Richard Tipping Salter who died on the 25th November 1891 in Cheltenham. A copy is as follows.

The obituary of Richard Tipping Salter by his brother Charles Salter as seen in the Baptist Visitor - 1900

The subject of this brief sketch was the son of Christian parents and staunch supporters of the Baptist Denomination. He was born at Wotton-under-Edge, the scene of the labours of the famous Rowland Hill, in the year 1814. Brought up in a Christian home, and amidst good influences, he responded early in life to the call of Jesus Christ, and was baptized by Mr. Watts, the Pastor of the Baptist Church at Wotton, and received into membership. He was apprenticed to the Tailoring and after serving his time came to Coleford about the year 1835. Here he married a Miss Jones, by whom his family, now living, was born. Some time after her death he married Miss Ann Morris, aunt of Mr. Ben Morris. She was an active Teacher in our Sunday School for many years. Tipping Salter was a strong believer in prayer, both public and private. He had family worship in the home, a custom which all Christian people will do well to follow, and which when neglected, is not only a loss to the home but to the Christian Church. After dinner every day he withdrew himself for a time of quiet communion with his God. So our friend's life was strong and healthy, being nourished by the secret springs from the presence of the Most High. Mr. Salter for many years was a local preacher, and rendered service to congregations meeting at Parkend, Redbrook, Penalt, Symond's Yat, and several other places as opportunity offered. He was also a member of our Choir, from the time of his coming to Coleford till he left. In June, 1884, he removed to Cheltenham and attended Salem Baptist Church, under the Pastorate of the Rev. R.G. Fairbairn, B.A., where he remain till his death, which took place November 25th 1891, at the age of 77.

Charles Salter was on the Committee to provide funds by an appeal to celebrate the Coronation of Their Majesties King Edward V11 and Queen Alexandra on the 26th June 1902. Charles would have been 89 years of age at this time. He was also involved in various Charities. We read in Cyril Hart's informative Book on the History of Coleford that an Indenture dated 21st December 1892 from Isaiah Trotter, J.P. of the Coombs, to the Reverend William Ross of Coleford, the Minister of the Baptist Church. Charles also has mention in this book. Isaiah Trotter on 28th April 1899 made a donation of £8,000 for the upkeep of the Almshouse by a Declaration of Trust. The Minister was the Reverend Arthur Horlick and one of the eight Deacons was that of Charles Salter. Cyril Hart also gives mention of various traders and includes Charles Salter and Son (Tailors) of the Market Place off Newland Street dated 1914. There are also a number of photo prints in various publications that may be seen in the Coleford Library, especially that of Humphrey Phelps that shows a family photo of Charles and his son Hubert James Salter. The following are photo's taken from the Family Archives. Because of the delicate nature of the photographs they have been reproduced.

Picture on left is of Charles & Sophia Salter
Picture on right is Hubert James & his father Charles Salter

As mentioned above, Isaiah Trotter, J.P. was of the Coombs House, Sparrows Hill in Coleford. It may be of interest that this House became a Nursing Home. Molly Manifold was the niece of William Trull & Julia (nee Jones) Salter that has mention on page114/115. She was born on 4th September 1912, the daughter of Hubert Gwilliam (born about 1880 in the district of Newland, Coleford in Gloucestershire. She married Desmond Manifold. They lived in Boxbush Road, Coleford, and after the death of Desmond she remained at Boxbush Road premises until her illness when she eventually took up residence at the Coombs Nursing Home. She died there on the 24th July 2003 and from there went to the Forest of Dean Crematorium on the 31st July 2003 where her remains were scattered in the picturesque landscape. The author is very much indebted to Molly for her kindness and help in the compiling of the Family history and the introduction to cousins now living in the Cardiff area of South Wales, namely Tyann (nee Salter) and Rev. Peter Leonard.

5.   Joseph Salter, the youngest son of Richard & Harriet (nee Jones) Salter, was born in December 1849 at the Poolway in Coleford and he died in April 1939 at 1 High Street, Westbury in Gloucestershire and he was interned on the 22nd April 1939 in Coleford Cemetery at the age of 89 years. He married Eliza, the daughter of George Whittaker of Coleford, on the 26th July 1873 at the Baptist Chapel, Newland Road in Coleford. Eliza died at High Nash and she was buried on 6th February 1922 in Coleford Cemetery. He probably did his apprenticeship with Gwilliam & Company of Bank Street who was Painters and Decorators. He would have been cousin to Molly Manifold through William Trull Salter who married Julia Jones. Julia's sister, Eva Jane Jones married Hubert Gwilliam the father of Eveline Molly Manifold. The details of his descendents may be seen in the Salter Archives from 1211.

The Salter family of Coleford originated from Cheshire and Shropshire in the Salt Mining districts and they are first recorded as far back as 1211 where they are mentioned in the Shrewsbury Abbey Records. As we have seen in earlier Chapters the families moved to 20 different Counties within the United Kingdom. The branch that is associated with Coleford moved to Dorset, Devon and Cornwall and we see later generations moving into Somerset, Gloucestershire and Wiltshire. Some were to become involved in the Textile trades whilst others were trading in the Food Trade. Although Richard Tipping Salter was the first to leave Kingswood near Wotton-under-Edge for the Forest of Dean in Gloucestershire in the 19th century there is a record of a Roger Salter living in the Newland district of Coleford in the 17th century. The name of the Property was "Paingree" and the tenant was a Chris Morgan, reference- (PRO-MR 879). A reference is also made in Cyril Hart's Book on the History of Coleford. However, there is no certain connection with the Salter's' now living and the Salter's' of the 17th century in Coleford.

Cyril Hart, in his History of Coleford also gives reference to the Teague family.

The Teague family lived at the Poolway and opposite to that of Richard Tipping Salter and his family. The two families were to become close friends and Edward Teague who was born about 1773, was to marry Lucy Prosser. They were ancestors of Julia Jones who was born 26th March 1870, and her sister Minnie Jones who was born 9th November 1879. Please see the Ancestor and Descendent Charts on Page 115. Peter Teague who was of the next generation was witness to the wedding of Richard and Harriett, the daughter of George and Eleanor Jones, on the 29th May 1837. The Teague's were in the Tin Mining business where some of the Salter's worked. Some of the Davies families were also associated with Tin Mining and Robert Davies became the Manager at Lydbrook. Thomas Teague family became Auctioneers in Coleford and Lydney. They were to auction the furniture and effects of Hubert James Salter, the Son of Charles and Sophia (nee Howell) Salter, and the twin of William Trull Salter, at 46 Newland Street on Thursday, 23rd September 1920, prior to their emigration to New Zealand. The Salter and Teague families have mention in the Trade Directories of the 19th century.

William Salter, who has mention above, purchased a property at the corner of Saint John Street and Boxbush Road, Coleford. Adjacent to Saint John Street was the old Tram Line that ran up to the corner of Boxbush Road. A photo of the Corner Shop may be seen on the next page with William and his son George Salter standing in the doorway. In 1951 George Salter sold the premises to a fishmonger. However, within eighteen months the property was once again sold. Brian Raymond, who also had premises in Lydney, purchased the property in 1953 where he opened the premises as general stores selling good quality clothing; footwear, and haberdashery. At the side of the shop was a room that had been used as a sowing room. However, Brian Raymond extended this to incorporate this room as the main shop. Outside is a yard that is the site of the old Mine Shaft. It was considered that the mine be re-opened in the early part of the 20th century. However it was not possible to re-open due to the fact that the local refuse had filled in the mine and therefore the venture did not succeed. It was also considered by the then Council that it would be too near to the existing shop premises. Nevertheless the exact location to the entrance to the old mine is not certain without digging up the whole area. The yard is now used for deliveries of goods to Raymond's Stores. At the rear of the yard is a Garage come Workshop. Brian Raymond has been very helpful concerning the history of the Stores and that of the Salter family during the mid 19th century to the mid 20th century when we see the last male line ending with George Salter who had continued his father's business in Boxbush Road, Coleford. Brian guided me by way of contacts for further research and I am very grateful for his help and hospitality.

*Standing in the doorway of No.1 Boxbush Road, Coleford
is William Salter with his son George Frederick Salter*

Picture showing the rear of No.1 Boxbush Road on the right and in the centre of the Picture is the Independent Chapel
On the left and opposite No.1 is where Jonah Slade and family lived.

Picture taken in 1997 showing Brian Raymond standing outside his shop premises at 1 Boxbush Road with Melvyn Salter

*Picture of Eric & June Bradley and Keith I. Davies a descendent of the
Salter Family out side number 30 Boxbush Road in Coleford*

George Salter died on the 8th November 1953 at the age of 75 and he was interned at Coleford Cemetery on the 12th November 1953. The Rev. Chilvers conducted the Service. George's wife Caroline died four years later at the age of 78 on Christmas Day, 25th December 1957 and she was interned on the 30th December 1957 in Grave No. SDN 29.

Many traders including that of George Salter and Mr. Ken Prisk supported the all male 'Splinters' Amateur Revue Company. The Salter family were close friends of Ken Prisk's father who lived at Lords Hill, Coleford. The Salter's and the Prisk families would spend many an enjoyable evening playing billiards and Snooker at Lords Hill with their pipes and glasses of merry refreshments. Ken Prisk Junior was a musician. He would entertain his family and friends and he was known as a composer of music. This musical connection between the two families, the Salter's were also known for their musical talents, were no doubt one of the friendship ties that had been cultivated over the years. They were also members of the Baptist denomination and they were members of the Amateur Dramatic Societies of which George Salter took part. Ken died in 2002 leaving his wife, Vera and family. Vera still lives in the family home at Lords Hill.

Another person who was associated with the Salter family was Win Watkins of whom I am greatly indebted for her kindness in helping me fill in the gaps with regard to my family history and introducing to my cousins Vicky Stackhouse (nee Salter) who now lives in Hereford. She was also musical and she often played the Organ in the Baptist Church in Newland Street, Coleford and she would be invited to play at other Churches in the area of the Forest of Dean. She died in 2001 leaving a sister who still lives in Coleford and a brother who lives with his family on the South Coast. She once told me that she could remember the days when she worked for George Salter at his Drapery Shop in Boxbush Road. She was a seamstress and shared the work with another drapery assistant to George Salter. The two ladies would sit (as did my grandfather, Alfred Salter) perched cross-legged on the tailoring bench. The room that was used for this purpose was situated in a sowing room at the side of the premises that is now incorporated into the main shop premises.

The first son Richard (known as Rowland Hill and named after the Rev. Rowland Hill of Wotton-under-Edge) and Hubert, the author's great-grandfather, of Richard Tipping and Harriett (nee Jones) Salter also became apprentice tailors to their father. Rowland remained in Coleford until the later part of the 19th century. He was born in 1838 at the Poolway and he later married Agnes, the daughter of James Wintle, a coalminer, in 1863. Agnes died at the Poolgreen, Coleford at the early age of 43 after she had bore five children, four boys and one girl, Harriet (the twin of Frederick) who died young and she was buried on the 28th August 1873 in Coleford Cemetery. Rowland married his second wife Ann and by 1901 they had moved to Uttoxeter that is near Burton-on-Trent in Staffordshire.

Hubert, the second son of Richard Tipping and Harriett (nee Jones) Salter, moved to Bristol where he married Martha, the daughter of Benjamin Trotman of Stonehouse in Gloucestershire, on the 5th September 1864 at Saint Matthias Church near the Weir and the Castle Precinct in Bristol. However, after his children were married and had left Bristol for South Wales he moved back to Coleford where he is buried. He died at Monmouth Hospital on the 21st March 1912 and was buried on the 24th March 1912 in Coleford Cemetery, Grave H29D.

Another Salter that was connected with Boxbush Road was Emma Louisa, the daughter of Charles & Sophia Salter. She was born in 1865 and married Henry Marsh, a baker by trade, in 1892. They lived in William Salter's house in 30 Boxbush Road where their first two children were born. After their third child was born they moved to Wolverhampton. The family were Baptists and although they had moved to Wolverhampton, Henry Marsh still kept in touch with Coleford Baptist Church and remained an active member of the Wotton-under-Edge Baptist Church. Their daughter, Margaret was born in Coleford and when Charles's wife Sophia died she returned to Coleford and stayed with her uncle for a time before she moved to a flat in the Clifton area of Bristol where the family of Ruth and Richard Dent were living.

A picture of Margaret Marsh taken in 1960 – This picture was sent with a Christmas Greeting to Christine & Stan Cook in Australia

Stan Cook was born in 34 Boxbush Road, Coleford in 1915 and a few doors away from 30 Boxbush Road where William and Eliza (nee Furney) lived. Next door to the Cook's residence was the new property numbered 32a. George Salter had this bungalow built for himself and his wife Caroline (nee Morgan) in 1912. They had no children.

At the age of 21 Stan Cook went to work in London but remembers that his father and mother were good friends of the Salters and he would have known briefly the friendship of the Prisk family at Lords Hill. He remembers that William Salter showed him how to write with both hands at the same time with the writing going in opposing directions, i.e. "mailliW William." Stan's father was born in Berkley. He married the daughter of Jonah Slade who lived at number 4 Boxbush Road and opposite to William Salter's Drapery & Tailor Shop. Jonah Slade was born in Rowde, near Devizes in Wiltshire in 1841. He came of strong Baptist stock and his mother's maiden name was Packer-Chivers who came from Lydiard Millicent near Swindon in Wiltshire. In the latter part of 1850 he migrated to the Forest of Dean and after being in Cinderford and Lydney where his early family were born, settled in Coleford.

According to the 1881 census Jonah Slade was a draper's assistant. At the time he worked for a business in the town, although later he set up on his own as a journeyman draper, and operated from his home address. Kelly's Directories for 1894 and 1897 give him as "Jonah Slade, draper, of Boxbush Road" and in 1910 and 1923 as a "woollen draper". Stan's father was a member of the Congregational Church in Berkeley that is situated in the northern side of Wotton-under-Edge and the Stroud Valley. The Cook family would have known the Itinerant Preacher, Charles Salter and Rev. Rowland Hill, who would have preached in their Church and the surrounding districts. Stan had been brought up as a member of the Independent Church that is opposite the bottom end of Boxbush Road and can be seen in the Photo on page 121. Stan's father became ill in the early 1920's and as a result of his illness became bedridden until he died in 1928. After the death of his father, Stan was welcomed into the Baptist Church in 1830 where Charles Salter was Deacon of that Church and Richard Tipping Salter was a Lay-Preacher. The fact that Stan's mother was of the Baptist persuasion and the Salter's influence in that regard that he was to become a member of the Baptist Congregation.

Jonah married Eliza Amelia Rice in 1863 and she became known as Amelia. She was born in Lydney but her ancestral origins were of the Bristol area. Amelia died in 1915, but fortunately they had both had the joy of celebrating their Golden Wedding, on Wednesday, 20th August 1913. There is an account of that event in the "Dean Forest Guardian" of the 22nd August 1913 in which appears the following – "At the luncheon which was provided, several old friends of the family were also present, including Mr. Charles Salter (who, it will be remembered had the good fortune to celebrate his diamond wedding in February of last year."

A photo of Jonah & Amelia Slade to celebrate their 50 years Golden Wedding at Coleford on the 20th August 1913

Front Row is the Slade Family
Back Row is the Salter Family – from left to right –
1   2   3   4 William 5   6 Charles 7 Sophia 8   9 Maude 10   11
George Frederick 12 Caroline

A photo of Charles & Sophia Salter showing four generations and in celebration of their Diamond Wedding in 1912

A Picture of Victoria Street in Coleford
and at the top of the street is the cemetery

The two Salter brothers, Richard Tipping and Charles Salter became successful in their profession as Master Tailors and as a result of their successes apprenticed their children in the trade. Some daughters of each family became seamstresses while some of their sons were apprenticed to their father as tailors. Although the trade was good within the Forest of Dean there would not have been enough work for the whole families especially as the third generation also took up the profession. Therefore it became inevitable that the tailors in the family were to move out of the area in search of work and less competition.

Of the two families some went to Bristol, while others went to South Wales and some even emigrated to New Zealand. In the next Chapter we shall see where the descendents of the two brothers sought their fortune and livelihood.

This Property at the Poolway that was owned by Peter Teague and let to his friend, Richard Tipping Salter and his wife Harriet nee Jones– a Master Tailor – was said to be a hum of activity with women Seamstresses going about their business. It was the Salter family home from 1837.

Opposite this property is Poolway House that is now a Hotel & Guest House and behind it is the Poolway Farm that was the home of the Teague Family for many generations. It is said that Charles 1 went into hiding there after the battle of Worcester and before his escape to France in 1623. The Kings aid was a John Peeters of Horton who had married Mary Salter of Devon. There is a Well at the rear of Poolway House and it has become known as "King Charles's Well".

This property and known as No.16 Gloucester Road, Coleford was the home of Richard Tipping Salter and his second wife Anne Morris in the 1860's

A picture of Charles & Sophia Salter and family

From Left to Right – Standing – William Trull and wife Julia (nee Jones) Salter, their two daughters, Edith (nee Young) & her husband Hubert James Salter

Charles Salter's shops – No.10 & 17 St. John Street,- Melvyn Salter in Picture

Photo of Market Place where Charles Salter had his Drapery & Tailoring business during the later part of the 19th century and the 20th century – as seen from Saint John Street

Picture of the Old Clock Tower (the only remaining structure of the Church) in Market Place, Coleford

The first picture shows the continuation of Market Place just below the Church Tower and leading to Newland Street in Coleford

Second picture shows the row of shops opposite the first picture and the Odds & Ends Shop is where Molly Manifold (nee Gwilliam) was born in Coleford

Chapter Eleven

:::::::::::::::::::::::::::::

The extended family spread their wings once again and move into Bristol, South Wales, The Northern Counties, New Zealand, Australia and Canada

Although the means of transport in the 18th century was by road and the use of horse and carriage to transport goods and persons, other means of transport was soon to follow. However, in 1759 Canals were built in order to move heavier goods such as Coal, Timber and Tinplate. It was by 1782 that Watt had invented and built a steam engine that was to revolutionize the method of transport. Stephenson was to follow Watt in the development of Steam Power by building the first locomotive in 1814. And by 1825 the first railway between Stockton and Darlington was opened. It was not long before other rail links were established across the United Kingdom.

We have seen in previous Chapters that families moved around the Country in order to find work. The 19th century was no exception but the big difference was the means of transport. While some families still used the old method of the Coach and Horses up until the 20th century the advantage of steam travel made it easier for poorer persons to move about the Country. And with the decline in the Cloth Industry it became necessary for families to seek there fortunes elsewhere. Some who were making their living by mining coal or tin where to move to new Mining districts. Other families who were associated with Sheep farming and the Woollen and Textile Industries were to retain a link with the Industry by becoming Tailors.

In the mid 19th century Scotland was producing fine suits and clothing. In 1848 we see that Peghouse Mill near Stroud in Gloucestershire was producing yearn for the Scottish market. An article was written in the Gloucester Journal dated 15th January 1848 concerning this product of Wool and Cloth for tailoring. A firm that was based in Trowbridge, Wiltshire, was that of Samuel Salter who had exhibited 150 varieties of Trousers together with Coats and other woollen tailored products. He had also produced silk garments that had won him a gold medal. The British Commissioners had produced a favourable report on the Paris Exhibition of 1878 where traders from Bristol and the surrounding areas within Wiltshire and Gloucestershire were producing good quality suits and clothing. However it was stated that there were less men seeking to obtain suits direct from their tailors. This could be proved wrong when we see the Salter families of the West Counties thriving in the Tailoring and Drapery businesses.

We can trace three generations of tailors from the 1830's to the 1950's doing well in the trade.

Perhaps the statement above was the fact that there were firms that had started making ready made suits and it is fact that this was proving a competition within the tailoring trade. However by the second world war the method of producing ready made suits did become popular and we can see this in the successful firm of Burtons that eventually were opening up shops in every major town and city within the U.K.

One example of a family deciding to move from a district in order to seek their fortune elsewhere because of too much competition is that of the Salter family.

The two brothers who were born in Kingswood, Wiltshire and the sons of Jacob and Mary (nee Trull) Salter that has mention in previous Chapters had moved across the Severn estuary to Coleford in the Forest of Dean, Gloucestershire and they had become successful Drapers and Tailors. However their sons and daughters were apprenticed to the tailoring trade. Although they too had become successful under the supervision and wing of their respective fathers they were finding that they needed to settle elsewhere in order to prosper.

We find that the only branch of the family in Coleford to remain trading there until the 1950's was the nephew of Richard Tipping and Charles Salter, William Salter and the son of John and Elizabeth (nee Pick) Salter, Clothier of Wotton-under-Edge and North Nibley, Gloucestershire. William Salter was apprenticed to his uncle Charles at the age of 14 in 1861 and as is mentioned previously remained in Coleford until his death. His son George Frederick Salter, who produced no heir, died in 1953 and thus the family of tailors in Coleford ended with that of George Frederick Salter.

The first of the Salter family to depart from Coleford was Hubert Salter, the great grandfather of the author and the second son of Richard Tipping & Harriett Salter. He was apprenticed to his father and after his apprenticeship he moved to Bristol in Somerset. He first lived at the Narrow Weir near the Castle Precinct. He married Martha Trotman who was born in Stonehouse in Gloucestershire at Saint Matthias Church near to the City Centre of Bristol on 5th September 1864. After their marriage they moved to the Saint James Church Yard Cottages where Hubert's cousin Alderman George Cole lived. Hubert Salter had his drapery business in Saint James. Hubert and Martha Salter's children were born here. However, Martha was not a strong women and it was with much sadness that she lost some of their children at an early age. Their were two sons who lived beyond the age of 10 years and they were Hubert Tipping Salter, their first born and Alfred Salter. Both Hubert Tipping and his brother Alfred were apprenticed to their father Hubert. During this period Bristol was situated within two Counties of Gloucestershire and Somerset. It may be of interest here to mention that Saint James, Bristol was and still is in the County of Gloucestershire.

Martha, partly due to her producing sickly children became very ill and depressed, and eventually it became too much for her to bear. She was later admitted to a psychiatric hospital in Stapleton area of Bristol or as was termed in the 19th century an asylum. After ten years of suffering she died peacefully on the 22nd March 1896 in the presence of her family. If she had lived in the 20th century then she would have been helped to overcome her depressed state of mind after the loss of some of her children. However, Hubert remained a devoted husband and he would visit her daily and he remained with her during her final hours before she departed this life to a better one with her maker. When Martha was taken ill, Hubert moved with his son Alfred and lived at 6 Lower Church Lane, St. Michaels that is situated above Christmas Steps and above St. James Parish of Bristol. They are recorded in the 1891 census. Alfred Salter married Minnie Ada Jancey and they lived at this address until the family moved to Cardiff in South Wales in the early part of 1900. According to the 1901 census they were recorded as still living at 6 Lower Church Lane. However, Hubert had moved to a new address in Bristol, No.3 Park Place. Ellen Victoria Jancey, the mother in-law of Alfred Salter was living at No.9 Park Place with her grand daughter Rosalie Ellen Salter, age 2

Alfred Salter married Minnie Ada, the daughter of Edmund Daniel Jancey on the 24th December 1894. After the birth of their fourth child, Charles Arthur Salter on 11th May 1901, the family moved to 3 Merthyr Street in Cardiff, South Wales. Another member of the family to move to South Wales was Minnie's sister, Phoebe Ellen Jancey. She had moved to Ynyshir, Pontypridd in Mid Glamorgan from Bristol where she married Ernest Francis Farleigh of Devon on the 22nd October 1892. Their daughter Annie Matilda Farleigh was born 21st March 1896 at Cymer in Mid Glamorgan. Annie moved to Cardiff where she married Mr. Saunders who died at sea during the First World War of 1914 to 1918. She later married her second husband Charles Brown. They had one son Charles who married Joyce who now lives in the family home in Canton, Cardiff. Annie died in the same year as her cousin Rosalie Ellen (nee Salter) Davies, on the 14th November 1975 at St. David's Hospital, Cardiff. However, on the marriage Certificate of Ernest Farleigh and Phoebe Jancey there are a few errors namely Phoebe was spelt incorrectly and spelt as 'Phebe'. Also it reads the father of Phoebe as Edward instead of Edmund Daniel Jancey.

Alfred Salter
(6/8/1871 to 30/8/1951)

ANNIE MATILDA (nee FARLEIGH) BROWN
(21/3/1896 TO 14/11/1975)

Rosalie Ellen (nee Salter) Davies with son Keith

Alfred Salter's wife, Minnie Ada (nee Jancey) Salter died at the early age of 37 in 1907, and it was after the war years between 1918 and 1920 that he and the family moved from Cardiff to live at 5 Victoria Place in Newport, Monmouthshire. While living there he became a member of the BUFFS Organisation. The BUFFS quarters were situated on the main Cardiff Road and one evening there was to be a dinner. Alfred went to this official dinner dressed, as was the custom, in dinner suit with tails. Because it was only about a mile from his house he walked. On his return he heard footsteps behind him and suspecting that there were some evil intent he thought quickly, turned and as he did so he lifted the tail of his suit with his hand holding his Silver Mounted Briar Pipe. It was a moon light night and to all it would appear that he had produced a Pistol whereby the attackers fled for fear that it was a revolver pointed straight at them. Alfred later wrote a brief note on the incident that read – "But what would they have thought had they known that my revolver was nothing more or less than my Silver Mounted Briar Pipe – The Motto – 'He that hesitates is lost'.

A hand written note by Alfred Salter

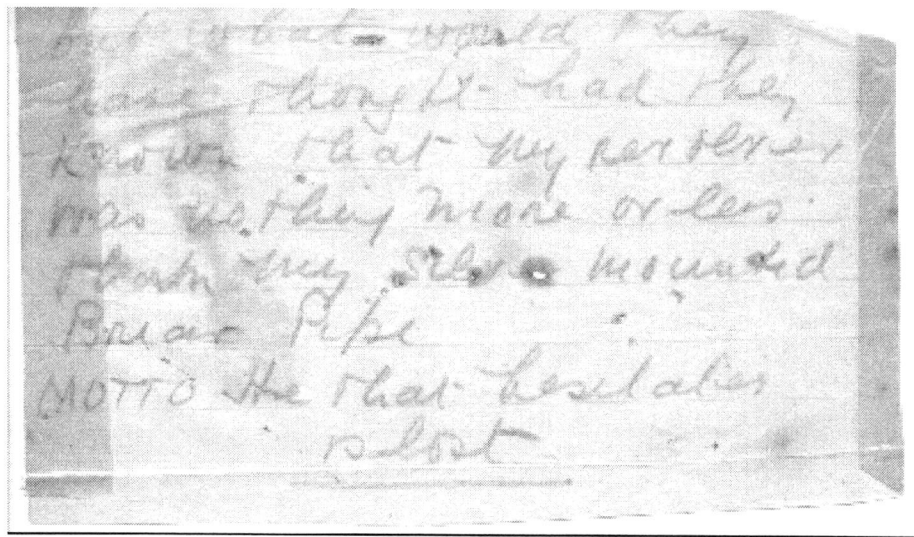

A picture showing No.3 Park Place, Clifton in Bristol where Hubert Salter & his sister Selina Salter lived during 1894 and 1902

No.9 Park Place, Clifton in Bristol, where Ellen Jancey and her two year old granddaughter Rosalie Ellen Salter were living in 1901

The second member of the Salter family to move away from Coleford was Selina, the daughter of Richard Tipping and Harriet Salter. She moved to Cheltenham as a house servant and later became a landlady where she took in lodgers at 8 Bath Parade. The row of houses from 1 to 8 have since been demolished and replaced by a car park. After the death of Richard Tipping Salter's second wife Ann he moved to Cheltenham where he lived with his daughter in 1884 and he remained there until his death on 25th November 1891. Sometime after the death of her father she moved to 3 Park Place in Bristol where her brother, Hubert Salter had moved during the mid 1890. Hubert Salter's granddaughter, Rosalie Ellen Salter (age two years) was living with her grandmother, Ellen Jancey, the mother of Minnie Ada Salter at 9 Park Place and a few doors away from Hubert at 3 Park Place, Bristol. By the mid 1900 Hubert and Selina Salter moved back to their birthplace of Coleford in the Forest of Dean, Gloucestershire where they remained until their deaths. However, Hubert was admitted to Monmouth Hospital where he died in 1912 and he was interned at Coleford Cemetery.

William Trull Salter, the son of Charles and Sophie (nee Howell) Salter was apprenticed as a Printer and firstly moved from Coleford to Cheltenham in 1884 where his uncle Richard Tipping Salter and his cousin Selina Salter were now living. Within a few years he moved to Cardiff in South Wales to seek his fortune. His descendents are now living near Cowbridge, South Wales.

Hubert James Salter and the twin of William Trull Salter, was apprenticed to his father Charles as a tailor and he became a partner in Charles Salter's business until his father died in 1921. He and his family then moved to New Zealand where some of his sons also became tailors in the new frontier. Steven Hubert (known as Steve) Salter, the descendent of Hubert James Salter, was born in Vancouver, Canada where he is living now. His father was Frederick Charles Salter and he became known as Steve. He was born in Coleford in 1905. He trained in New Zealand as a Marine Engineer and he later travelled the world. He met the girl of his dreams in Vancouver, Kate McKinnon and they married in 1939. Steve died in Vancouver in 1998 leaving a son. His son, who was mentioned above, became a Financial Advisor and he later founded the firm "Fimetrics Systems Ltd.," as a software development enterprise concentrating on personal financial planning. He had previously had 35 years experience in the Computer Industry and he has a mathematics and engineering background. Some descendents of Hubert James and Edith nee Young Salter were apprenticed as tailors whilst others were associated to the medical profession and became Dentist. Donald Hubert John Salter, the grandson of Hubert James and Edith Salter, was born 1st June 1934 and he married Carol Williams on the 12th May 1962 at Dunedin in New Zealand. In about 1964 the family moved to Croydon in England where they carried on the profession as Dentists.

Richard and known as Rowland Hill Salter, the first son of Richard Tipping and Harriett (nee Jones) Salter became a tailor and he was apprenticed to his father. He remained in Coleford until the turn of the 20ᵗʰ century when he moved with his second wife Ann and their son Frederick who was born a twin in 1871 to Uttoxiter, near Burton-on-Trent in Staffordshire. Their other son Frank became a Coalminer and he moved with his family to Barnsley in Yorkshire.

It was not unusual for the descendents of the Salter families to become entrepreneur in the 20ᵗʰ century. Some became successful Butchers as is seen in Hubert Alfred Salter who established two shops in Kettering. Another was Victoria and known as Vicky (nee Salter) and her husband Phillip (Phil) Stackhouse who also acquired two Butcher shops in Hereford and Leominster and known as Hereford Butchers.

William Trull Salter was to establish a Printers business in Cardiff. Other members of the family were to take up Professions such as Engineers, Accountants, Dentists, and Artists.

Another entrepreneur was that of Carl Salter of Birmingham. He is the grandson of Charles and Evelyn (nee Watkins) Salter and the son of Melvyn and Philomena Salter. He started a successful cleaning business.

Picture of Charles & Evelyn (nee Watkins) Salter, the grandparents of Carl Salter and the father of Melvyn Salter

Carl & Maisie and Nicky & Millie
with Carl's father, Melvyn Salter

A portrait of Alfred Salter, the grandfather of Melvyn Salter and Keith Ivor Davies and father of Charles Salter & Rosalie Ellen (nee Salter) Davies

(On the back of this portrait reads "to my daughter Rosalie from her loving dad")

Chapter Twelve

....

The Salter family and their cousins converge on the City of Bristol

Throughout the centuries Bristol was a thriving port that brought various traders from numerous parts of the United Kingdom seeking work. The Salter's and their cousins were no exception. Some would seek their skills in shipping, finances as in stockbrokers and accountants, millers, bakers and various other commodities.

As we have seen in other Chapters the people of Bristol had their roots in Cornwall, Devon, Dorset and the Western parts of Somerset. Bristol was also the centre point where members of the family who had moved to foreign parts such as America and Canada would often return to visit their relatives and to explore their origins. One such adventurer may be seen in Mary Anne Cole of River View Cottage, North Nation Mills in Quebec.

During the summer of 1877 when Mary was just 17 years of age she was to travel by ship to England with her father. Her mother had instructed her to keep a daily account of her adventures in her diary. The full account of this may be seen at the Bristol Record Office. However, for those who are unable to travel to Bristol to view these records I will give extracts from her diary in order to try and explain some connections with other members of the family as in the names of Jancey, Salter, Bartlett, Farleigh and of course the Cole family.

When Mary and her father arrived in Bristol they took what was known as a four-wheeler to the premises of her uncle George Cole of 18 King Square in the Parish of Saint James and in the district of Clifton. George Cole was an Alderman of Saint James Parish. She writes in her diary, "On ringing the bell, the door was opened by a stately creature in knee breaches and black silk stockings. I was wondering to myself if that were some of our relations but on Papa's asking if the family were at home, I began to suspect it was a manservant. He took us up a flight of stairs, through a hall hung with pictures and carpeted with crimson carpet and opening the door of a room, called out 'Miss Cole and Mr. Cole' and so we were ushered into the presence of George Cole'. Uncle George is a fine looking man as straight as an arrow with silver white hair and black eyes. He has side-whiskers and is a most imposing looking personage. He always wears a little black velvet cap in the house. We were most heartily welcome; and Uncle

George kissed Papa – it seemed queer to see two men kiss each other. Auntie (Elizabeth) is just an old darling though at first glance she looked so very stately and unapproachable.

She wears a most wonderful cap – but she is just as kind as she can be. Auntie Walters was there spending the evening – she has blue eyes and curly brown hair and though she is 50 – looks twenty years younger. Then there was cousin Bessie, Uncle George's daughter – tall and blond and cousin Lucy – uncle William Cole's daughter who lives at Uncle George's. She has reddish brown hair and is a most motherly girl. I guess she must be nearly 30. Then there is little George (Henry) Salter – uncle George's grandson who is an orphan, his Mother and Father both having died. George will be a rich man if he lives to be twenty one."

George Henry Salter, the son of Henry Salter was born in 1865 and in the following year Hubert Tipping Salter, the son of Hubert & Martha Salter of Saint James, was born. They attended the same school in Saint James in Bristol. The Salter families were also members of the Baptist Church in Bristol. George married his cousin Jane Elizabeth, the daughter of Thomas Joseph Cole on 11th June 1890 at Tyndale Chapel in White Ladies Road in the district of Barton Regis (Clifton) that was then in the Counties of Bristol & Gloucestershire. He was trained as a Commercial Clerk and later became Manager of his father-in-laws Boot & Shoe Factory. However, he was to die young with T.B. at the age of 42. At the time of his death on the 28th September 1908 he was living at 66 Woodstock Road, Redland, Clifton Bristol. His sister-in-law, Edith was in attendance. Edith was residing at Esmond Victoria Buildings in Weston Super Mare in Somerset. Hubert Tipping Salter became a tailor and he was apprenticed to his father, Hubert Salter of Saint James. His last known address was 'Rowden House' Pilgrim Street in Newcastle-on-Tyne as per his letter to his father. According to his brother Alfred Salter who was born on 6th August 1871 at Saint James in Bristol, he had gone to live abroad. No further information is available except for a letter that is printed in the book entitled, "Salter Archives from 1211" by Keith I.E. Salter-Davies.

Phoebe Ellen Jancey, the daughter of Edmund (sometimes called Edward)& Ellen Jancey (of Old Sodbury) and the sister of Minnie Ada Salter, was born 1872 in Bristol and she married Ernest Farleigh, on the 22nd October 1892 in the Parish of Ynyshir, Pontypridd in Mid Glamorgan, South Wales. Phoebe was a first cousin to Rosalie Ellen (nee Salter) Davies through their paternal grandparents Edmund & Ellen Jancey of Bristol. The Farleigh families were connected with Newton Abbott that is near Denbury and also Dawlish in South Devon.

There are some interesting accounts of Mary's stay in Bristol that relate to other districts of Bristol that are associated with other members of the Salter families who are not mentioned in the diary but who are relevant when referring to the Families connections with Devon.

Firstly, before we start on further extracts of Mary's Diary, we may see the following pictures that were taken in 1998. The first shows the Saint James School Plaque and the second shows Keith, the author, standing on the top of Christmas Steps, the Saint Michaels parish of Bristol within the district of Clifton. At the bottom of these steps is Saint James's Parish.

After a late night talking and exchanging general chitchat they retired to bed. The next morning events are now related in the diary. "It is nearly nine o'clock and an hour ago a girl, a maid I suppose they call them here, brought me a cup of chocolate before I got up as Auntie thought I might be fatigued and would like something before dressing. I acted as if I were used to having chocolate brought to me every morning. The girl said the breakfast bell would ring at nine o'clock so I got up and dressed and am waiting for the bell to ring. I heard a rap at my door and Georgie was there wanting a kiss and said I was to go with him to Cousin Bessie's room so we went and found her combing her hair – sitting before the dressing table. She has lovely long hair that looks like floss silk. I noticed she had a cup of chocolate too. Georgie said to her 'Bessie, what will you give for what I have got' and then handed her a letter he had got from downstairs after opening the mailbox. It was a letter from her intended who is away for some weeks in Scotland and she gets a letter from him every morning. That is a lover such as you read of – His name is Harry Pockson. She has been engaged to him about eight months and they expect to be married next summer. He and his brother have a large factory outside of Bristol. She told me all this in quite a matter of fact manner. Then we went to breakfast and after that Uncle George and Papa went out and I was shown over the house with Cousin Lucy. There are four servants, Morgan the man with the calves – he waits on the door at night and at the dinner table and drives the carriage in the afternoon. There are two housemaids and a cook. The maids wait on the table and one waits on the door in the daytime. The house is large. There is a big hall, reception room and dining room, another long hall and then another room, then the kitchen downstairs – upstairs- on the first landing is a big hall, drawing room, dressing room – Auntie's bedroom and in a wing over the kitchen part is bathroom, closet and a couple of small rooms full of books and pictures. This is Uncle's 'Snuggery'. On the next landing are bedrooms and up again are the servant's rooms. Morgan sleeps somewhere down-stairs. Georgie and I have got on pretty friendly footing – he is a regular tease. ----- In the evening, Papa, Uncle George, Bessie and I went out in the carriage for a drive. Morgan, who had on a pair of pants by this time and a tall hat, drove the horses. We went past Clifton College where we saw the boys playing cricket – 'Cooks Folly' – under Clifton Bridge, Hotwells and around by the docks and then home just in time for tea and found Cousin Willie there. After tea we went for a walk and got home to supper at nine o'clock. On Sunday, 20th May (1877) we all went to the Independent Chapel and after dinner Cousin Lucy went to Sunday school in this Chapel where she is a teacher. Papa went with her and cousin Willie. Bessie went to service in Bristol Cathedral and in the evening went with Papa and cousin Sara and her husband Mr. Cummins and cousin Willie to King Street Baptist Chapel where the Cummins are members. The Minister made awful faces when he preached. Willie said he never could look at him, as for me I could not help looking at him."

It was not uncommon for families in the 19th century to practise their faith in different denominations. As we have so far seen from Mary's diaries that the Cole and Salter family were tolerant and would join and share in the different theologies within the Christian faith and worship together. They would sometimes go to the established Church, the Church of England and at other times would pray together in the Baptist Churches. Mary's Uncle John and Aunt were members of the Baptist Church and on one occasion John and Papa went to Weston-super-Mare to a Baptist meeting. The Baptist Church in Bristol also had links with Coleford were Charles and Richard Tipping Salter were Deacons and Richard a Lay-preacher in and around Coleford. Hubert, the second son of Richard had moved to St. James's Parish in Bristol and his cousin William, the youngest son of John & Elizabeth Salter stayed with the family there for a couple of years in order to do his final apprenticeship as a tailor. Before he left Bristol for Aylesbury in Buckinghamshire in 1871 he married Eliza Furney at the Broadmead Baptist Meeting House on the 12th September 1871. Another connection with Bristol Baptists was the New Baptist Church in Wotton-under-Edge in Gloucestershire. William's uncles Charles and Jacob and the aunts and uncles on the Trull, Tipping, and Marsh relatives were to have close connections with Bristol Baptists.

On the right hand side of the Picture taken in 1998 is seen the Broadmead Meeting House situated on the 1st floor of the centre building. The Church in the background is Saint James Parish Church and alongside the Church that is now a shopping precinct was the Saint James Churchyard Cottages were the Salter and Cole families lived during the mid to the later part of the 19th century.

The Baptist Church at Rope Walk
In Wotton-under-Edge
(Indenture dated 16th July 1816 & Consecrated 1818)

The following is an extract from the Indenture of 1816.

This Indenture Triparties made the sixteenth day of July in the fifty sixth year of the reign of our Sovereign Lord George the third by the Grace of the United Kingdom of Great Britain and Ireland King Defender of the Faith and in the year of Our Lord One Thousand Eight Hundred and Sixteen between Abraham Owen late of Wotton-under-Edge in the County of Gloucester Clothier but now of Basing-Hill Street in the City of London of Blackwell Hall Factors of the first part John Cooper of Wotton-under Edge aforesaid Surgeon of the second part and Samuel Long of Kingswood in the County of Wiltshire a Clothier Thomas Ovenbury of Nailsworth in the County of Gloucester a Clothier Henry Page of the City of Bristol a Baptist Minister James Griffiths of Wotton-under-Edge aforesaid a Baptist Minister William Perrin of Kingswood aforesaid a Clothier Jacob Salter of the same place a Cloth Worker-Engineer Joseph Rodway of Wotton-under-Edge aforesaid a Pawnbroker Benjamin Foxwell of the same place a Yeoman Samuel Povey of

Charfield in the said County of Gloucester an Engineer Joseph Foxwell of Wotton-under-Edge aforesaid a Weaver Uriah Foxwell of the same place a Tailor and Joseph Trull of Uley in the said County of Gloucester a Pig Butcher of the third part

Whereas in and by a certain Indenture of Feoffment of three parts with livery and seis'in thereupon indorsed bearing date on or about the Twenty-Ninth day of September in the year of Our Lord One Thousand Eight Hundred and Eight and made between Hamilton Green Parslow of the first part the said Abraham Owen of the second part and the said John Cooper of the third part All that late Orchard or Piece of Meadow or Pasture Ground but which was then converted into and used as a Garden which in the Parish of Wotton-under-Edge aforesaid lying at the back of certain Messuages or Tenements and premises then of the said Hamilton Green Parslow and bounded as therein mentioned together with the free use and enjoyment of a certain Well of Water of the said Hamilton Green Parslow near to the aforesaid Messuages and Tenements And Also of a footway or passage leading from the High Street of Wotton-under-Edge aforesaid up to the said Orchard or piece of Garden Ground through and over the entry Court Yard and Premises there belonging in the said Hamilton Green Parslow lying between the same Premises and the said High Street except the free use and enjoyment by the said Hamilton Green Parslow his Heirs and Assigns of a Carriage or Passageway

The present Baptist Minister of Wotton-under-Edge from 2001 is the Revered Phil Butcher.

A Picture of Saint James's Church in Bristol

A picture of Alfred & Minnie Ada (nee Jancey) Salter

The entry in the diary of Monday 21st May 1877 makes me consider the health problems that prevailed throughout the 19th century especially that of Consumption and T.B. I quote – "Papa and I went out to Uncle John's and stayed to dinner. They have dinner at six o'clock. Auntie is in very poor health and is a very lovely woman. She lost her only daughter three months ago. She was married and had three children and Auntie has not got over the shock." My grandmother, Martha (nee Trotman) who has mention in previous Chapters, was a sick woman and she had lost a number of her children at an early age. Her second son Charles Arthur died within twelve months of his birth, leaving only two sons, Hubert Tipping (known as Bert) and Alfred Salter. She is buried in the Ridgeway Park Cemetery, Stapleton where her grandson Edward George Salter, the son of Alfred and Minnie Ada Salter, was buried at the early age of 13 months. Hubert Salter the husband of Martha first arrived in Bristol from Coleford in the early part of the 1860's.

The Saint Matthias Church on the Weir
"Ecclesiae Bristoliana, being views with letter-press descriptions of the Churches of Bristol...from drawings by John Willis"

(166)   5 April 1959: Wellington Road to narrow weir
        (the reverse of plate 165): Broad Weir in the distance.
        St. Mathias Church and School (1855) were demolished 1959.

(This Picture was drawn in the 1890's of St. Matthias Church in Wellington Road, Bristol and designed by John Norton, 1851 (also available at the Bristol Library is High Cross and Stapleton Church). The Church was demolished in 1950 and the school to the left of the Church survived until 1959 when the area was cleared for the Inner Circuit Road, Stratton Street is off right, and the chimney of the public baths peeps round the Church tower (For further information see "1956-1959", plates 165 and 166 that are held in Bristol Library).

The Weir and the Castle Precinct areas of Bristol would appear to be the first port of call for some of the Salter families from Devon and Gloucestershire. Hubert Salter who has mention moved to the Weir on his first arrival in Bristol. Another Salter family that have connections with Devon and Gloucestershire was Henry Salter, a baker by trade and who was born in Ottery St. Mary in Devon. He married Sarah Rosser from Coleford in Gloucestershire and they had their first child, Eliza born in the Castle Precinct. Henry and his sister Eliza Salter both came to Bristol from the Parish of Ottery-St. Mary in Devon in 1851. Their Pedigree from the later part of the 18th century is -

Christopher Salter married Elizabeth Sprat on 22nd October 1798 at Ottery St. Mary and they had the following children.

Christopher was born about 1798/9 & he married Martha Webber.
1. Mary Ann was christened 9th January 1800.
2. George was christened 30th October 1800.
3. Elizabeth was christened 13th January 1803.
4. Maria was christened 5th June 1805.
5. William was christened 14th October 1807.

Christopher, son of Christopher & Elizabeth (nee Sprat) Salter, married Martha Webber on 30th July 1823 at Ottery St. Mary and they had the following children.
1. Sarah was born 16th November 1823.
2. Eliza was born 10th December 1826. She remained single and later found as head of the household in the 1881 census of St. Philip & Jacob Parish within the City of Bristol.
3. Henry was born 28th September 1828. He moved to Bristol in 1851 where he married Sarah Rosser of Coleford in St. Peters Church within the Castle Precinct of Bristol on the June quarter of 1851 reference X1-236.
4. John was born 17th April 1831.

Part of the Diary gives mention to the district of Fishponds and Saint Mary Redcliffe Parish Church. In the following narrative we will see other family connections with that of Taunton in Somerset and Devon.

Jerome Salter was born 24th January 1781 of Samuel & Martha (nee Gray) Salter, in Honiton, Devon. (Samuel Salter married Martha Gray on 30th May 1774) Samuel is recorded in the earliest Directory of Devon as a Glazier (1793-1798). Their other known children were Samuel Wall christened 6th June 1775 and Richard christened 21st June 1787. He married Jane May on 16th October 1809.

Jerome was apprenticed to his father Samuel as a Glazier. He married Susanna Bicknell and by 1811 the family were living in St. Mary Redcliffe. Their children were George and John (twins) christened 25th December 1813 at Saint Mary Redcliffe and Margaret Bicknell was christened 25th December 1815 also at Saint Mary Redcliffe. Jerome died in the March quarter of 1845 aged 64 and his wife Susanna died between 1855 and 1859.

It is believed that Susanna, the wife of Jerome Salter, maiden name was Bicknell as it was her daughter's second name. It has been the tradition throughout the generations that the second Christian name is that of the mother's maiden name.

On Sunday the 27th May 1877 Mary writes in her diary – "Chapel this morning and tonight, Bessie, Harry, Willie and I went to St. Mary's Redcliffe – it is the largest Parish Church in the world. There are two beautifully wrought brass gates at one of the entrances."

The Parish of Saint Mary Redcliffe and Saint John in Bedminster, an adjourning Parish, has been the home of many of the Salter families from Devon in the first half of the 19th century. Jerome Salter we have already mentioned as living in Saint Mary Redcliffe so we will now consider the other family members from Devon.

John Salter was born in the Parish of Pitminster near Taunton in 1789. He married Sarah Pavey at Ottery St. Mary in Devon on the 4th November 1822 at the age of 33 years. John did his apprenticeship as a baker and soon after his marriage; he and his wife moved to Bristol and started a Bakery business in the Parish of Saint Mary Redcliffe. He has mention in the Trade Directories of 1835, 1845 and 1855 and also Pigots Directory of 1830. They had four children namely, Sarah Ann was born 7th July 1825; John was baptized 21st June 1827 but died young at the early age of 4 years on 25th July 1831; Elizabeth was born in 1829 and Catherine was born in 1830. Sarah, the wife of John died at the early age of 46 on the 25th January 1835. John and family were living at 20 Redcliffe Hill and his parents were John of Clayhidon in Devon and Mary (nee Moor of Pitminster). John Salter, senior married Mary Moor on 28th March 1777 recorded on the Parish registers as page 50 and the witnesses to the wedding were Thomas Valentine and John Hicks. The Salter family originated from Sanford and sometimes spelt as Sandford North West of Exeter in Devon.

Charles Salter, also of Devon, is recorded in the Pigot's Gloucestershire Directories of 1830 as a baker and living in Somerset Place within the Parish of Bedminster, Bristol. I have been able to trace his marriage and children's details from extensive search as follows.

A Charles Salter married Mary Allen at Plymtree in Devon on the 16th January 1811. (Charles is referred too as from Sanford). He was a baker by trade.

The children connected with this marriage is Henry born about 1816 and baptized at Ottery St. Mary on 18th February 1818. (Charles is referred too as of Alphington). Sarah Allen Salter was born 1820 at Honiton and married Giles Reynolds, a farmer, on the 1st June 1847 in the Parish Church of St. Sidwell, Exeter. George Allen was born in Bedminster, Bristol in 1823 and married Charlotte Louisa Marchant in the Registry

Office in Exeter on 25th December 1845. Annie Maria was born 1825 and she was baptized at Saint Mary Redcliffe in Bristol on 26th March 1826. According to the 1851 census she moved to Devon and lived with her sister Sarah Allen Reynolds. Charles died in Bristol in 1832 and as there is no record of his wife Mary living or dying in Bristol after 1841 it is presumed that she moved back to Devon to be at her son, George Allen Salter's wedding in 1845. Researchers, Margaret McGregor and Jenny Currell of the Bristol Record Office have given much help in this research.

Henry Salter was a baker by trade and he was born about 1816. His parents are as yet unknown but it is believed that they were a Charles and Mary Salter from Devon. In 1830 he was living in Saint John's Parish within Bedminster and only about a mile and half from Saint Mary Redcliffe the adjourning Parish. Charles and Mary Salter were also living in Saint John's within Bedminster at Somerset Place. The question is whether Henry lived at the same address. They would have known each other and it is possible that Henry was apprenticed as a baker with Charles Salter. Henry would have been 14 years when living in Bedminster and he would have been in the first year of his apprenticeship. Charles died in 1832 at the early age of 46 years. Now in 1837, when Henry was in his final year of apprenticeship he was working for Henry Procter. In 1835 Henry Procter became a partner with a Mr. Shoard, a meal man, corn and flour factors of 1 Bell Lane that is situated at the bottom end of Broad Street in the City Centre of Bristol. It was here that Henry was a baker and he would have been working at this Factory. Henry Procter, prior to his new partnership with Shoard, was a dealer in china, glass and Staffordshire ware, a wholesale and retailer. His business premises were at 29 Wine Street and his private residence in 1835 was 7 Guinea Street that is situated off Redcliffe Hill where John & Sarah Salter, bakers, lived. He also had a Factory that manufactured Glue and he was also a Rag & Bone merchant. His Factory was at Cathy in Redcliffe. His residence was at 9 West Street that is situated off Old Market Street in The Weir district of Bristol and near to the Castle Precinct. It was unfortunate that Henry became involved in a petty offence concerning a small portion of Glue and Henry Procter subsequently took him to Court. His Court hearing was on Friday 12th January 1838 and as a result he was sentenced to 7 years deportation to Australia. The Colonies needed professional persons in order to establish a state within the new Country of Australia. In America we see a similar situation but with slave labour. It was an easy way to recruit persons for the new world through the Courts.

Henry Salter had decided to remain in Australia as he saw the future prospects to be good. By the 1850's Henry had met is future bride and in 1853 he married Margaret Steed.

A picture of Henry Salter taken in Australia

1816 to 1892

𝒜 𝒫ICTURE of the 𝒟escendents of 𝓗ENRY 𝒮ALTER taken in the year 2003

Back Row: Gabriella Salter (nee Sakrouge), David Salter, Anne Bretherton (nee Salter) Jamie Bretherton
Middle Row: Shirley Salter (nee Morcom) Bertha Morcom (Shirley's mother), John Salter
Front Row: Alexandra Bretherton, Christopher Salter, Cassandra Salter, Ashleigh Bretherton

A picture of the Descendents of Henry Salter taken in the year 2003

The next part of Mary's diary refers to her visit to Devon with her Papa and begins on Sunday 5th June 1877. It begins – "We are in Papa's old home now – got here about 5 this afternoon – on the way at Teignmouth, Aunt Elizabeth met us and came down with us. At Newton (Abbot) Station we were met by uncle William. He is not a bit like Uncle George and Uncle John – he is a small man with reddish hair, lovely white skin and rosy cheeks and seems as spry as a boy. We took a landau and drove to Denbury which is three miles from Newton Abbott, a lovely drive with the lilacs, laburnums and hawthorns which are all along the road all in flower and the orchards too are all in flower also and the trees looked like great rose bushes. As soon as we entered the village the Church Bells began to ring in honour of a Cole coming home. I felt quite proud; the bells are always rung when any of the Uncles come down. The village folks say it is an honour to have any of the Cole's come back to Denbury for they have been an honour to the place. After we landed at Uncle Williams where we found cousin Jennie who is Uncle's house keeper and Pollie who is married and lives just across the way, waiting for us, tea was ready and after tea, Papa held quite a reception; all the old schoolmasters who were living in the village came to see him. Jennie keeps just one woman to do the rough work and the rest she does herself. This is a dear old house with great deep window seats and unexpected nooks and corners and winding stairs. It is not a very large house but has a few acres of lovely garden and orchard with an old stonewall around it covered with ivy. My bedroom overlooks the orchard and the scent of the apple blossoms is delicious."

After describing further events in the house at Denbury we continue to read from the diary of Monday 5th June 1877 we take up the events of that evening. "… In the evening we all went for a walk to the top of the hill and Uncle and I had a race over the Downs – he can run faster than I can. Then we came home by Mr. Elliot's who is a second cousin of Papa's and he had three wives – all sisters – married the whole family. He is very well off and has a lovely garden with some beautiful standard roses, which he takes great, pride in. He has three children all grown up. He is a Baptist and has built a small Chapel in the village and pays a Minister to come and preach every two weeks. This is a thorn in the Vicar's side, that dissenting Chapel. Although Uncle William is a churchman, he goes to the Baptist Chapel too often to please the Vicar who thinks Uncle should set a better example being one of the most influential parishioners. This Vicar is very high Church which Uncle does not approve of." The Salter families were connected to the Elliot family through marriage. One such marriage was between Christopher Salter to Grace Elliot at Rockbear near Exeter on 9th March 1761. The family later moved to Ottery St. Mary. Another Salter that was named Elliot Salter had connections with Devon, Somerset, Dorset, Buckinghamshire and Bath. He was an Admiral in the Royal Navy.

The next extract from the diary relates to more cousins of the Cole family and refers to the musical talents of the family and that includes the Bartlett family of Teignmouth and Torbay and the Salter families in general. (6th June 1877) "It is pouring this morning and quite chilly after a dreadful thunderstorm in the night so Jennie made a fire in the grate in the morning room and we sat there most of the day, Papa, Uncle and Aunt going over old times; Jennie working at some embroidery and read some old 'Argos's'. In the evening Walter Elliot and James Roe and Old Mr. Roe came in and we had music nearly all evening. Mr. Roe is a great violin player and we had quite a concert." (On the 9th June) "Attended an English wedding in the Church; bride 50 – groom 44 years. They have been engaged for 20 years. In the afternoon the Vicar and his wife called and want Papa and I to go up to tea some evening. After they left the Miss Gardners called from the Manor House – three old maids and very prim indeed. James Roe called after tea and we went for a walk to Tor-hill." (On the 11th June) " Aunt, Papa and Uncle went to South Moulton to see some of their cousins who live there." She goes on to say that the next day, the 12th June, they went down to 'Holwell Farm' and visited old Mr. & Mrs. Godfrey were they stayed all day and had a good time. The next entry is the 13th June. "We went down to Dawlish this morning – a lovely spot by the sea where cousin Edwin and his family live. Cousin Rose, his wife is a beauty with lovely auburn hair and brown eyes. They have three pretty children – two girls and a boy called Courtney – lovely yellow curls and big blue eyes." This boy was evidently named after the Courtney family as is mentioned in earlier Chapters. (On the 14th June) "This morning we took an open carriage and drove down to Torquay. Had tea at cousin Sara Travener's and drove around Saint Mary's Church, Brixham and Penton; Brixham famed for fish and Penton for cabbages. Then around Babbicombe Bay and home." (On 15th June) "This morning we drove out to Totness and had lunch in the ruins of Totness Castle and walked around what was left of the old Roman Wall and then to Berry-Pomeroy castle built in the time of William I." (On Sunday 17th June she writes) "This morning we went to Church and had the pleasure of seeing Sir Samuel Baker, the African traveller. He is staying at the Vicarage. He is a kind looking white haired old gentleman." (On Monday 18th June) "This morning Uncle, Cousin Edwin, Papa and I went to the Top of the Down, it was a beautifully clear morning and we could count the spires of nineteen Parish Churches from the Tip of the Down. Then we went down to 'Yet Farm' and had dinner with the Hallcrosses." (On Monday 25th June) "Papa and I went up to the Vicarage this forenoon and had lunch with Mrs. Reibey and then we went down to the gardens, which were lovely. I had a great bouquet to take home." (On Tuesday 26th June) "Drove down to Buckfast Leigh through Jersey and had lunch at the 'Kings Arms', then walked through the town up to Hannline House. The Hannlins have large Factories there. Then we went down to Ashburton where Auntie used to go to boarding school. Bought some of its famous cakes then drove home around Mead Hill."

Edwin and Rose Cole of Dawlish in Devon that has mention in the previous page and the entry of Mary's diary of 13ᵗʰ June 1877 was related to Ernest Farleigh who moved to Bristol and then to Pontypridd in South Wales where he married Phoebe Jancey of Bristol. Edwin Cole married Rosina (known as Rose) June Farleigh in Dawlish, Devon on 29ᵗʰ January 1872.

The Cole Family revisited their cousins in Saint Mary's Church that is now part of Torquay and I quote – "We all went down to Torquay again yesterday to some relatives of which there are a number. The older ones visited together quietly while we younger ones walked about seeing the sights."

The Salter and the Bartlett families were connected with Torquay, Dawlish, Plymouth, Saint Mary's Church, Totness, Denbury, Newton Abbott, Teignmouth, Ottery St. Mary, Exeter including Alphington and to the North of Exeter, Upton Pyon and Sandford or as it is sometimes called Sanford, Crediton, and we must not forget the Counties of Cornwall, Dorset, Somerset, Wiltshire and Gloucestershire. Throughout this short history of the family throughout the generations I have tried to give a general view of life and their occupations. However, there is much more that one could include but I will leave any further writings for another time. For anyone that may be interested a fuller account of the family trees may be seen in the forthcoming book entitled, "The Salter Archives from 1211". This book will be ready for publication by the mid 2005.

I have also included at the end of this book a list of writers and their book titles that may be of interest to those seeking a fuller knowledge of social and industrial culture in the West Counties.

Index

Recommended Further Reading

Title	Author
Gloucestershire Woollen Mils (1967)	Jennifer Tann
The Cloth Industry in the West of England from 1640 to 1880	J. De L. Mann
The Wiltshire & Somerset Woollen Mills	Kenneth H. Rogers
Sheep Bell and Ploughshare	Marjorie Reeves
Wotton-under-Edge – A Century of Change	Geoffrey Masefield
Cadfael Country	Rob Talbot & Robin Whiteman
Savouring The Past (The Droitwich Salt Industry)	J.D. Hurst
Saint Mary's Churchyard and Tomb Trail	John Cordwell
As Mad As A Hatter	David E. Evans
Salt and the Doomsday Salinae at Droitwich	Beatrice Hopkinson
Handbook of Dates for Students of English History	C.R. Cheney
Religion and Society in Cotswold Vale	Albion M. Urdank
Writing and Publishing Your Family History	John Titford
Chartism	Edward Royle